Favorite Christmas Quilts

~≈~ from That Patchwork Place ~≈~

Martingale
& COMPANY

Bothell, Washington

CREDITS

President . . . . Nancy J. Martin
CEO/Publisher . . . . Daniel J. Martin
Associate Publisher . . . . Jane Hamada
Editorial Director . . . . Mary V. Green
Design and Production Manager . . . . Cheryl Stevenson
Technical Editor . . . . Ursula Reikes
Copy Editor . . . . Liz McGehee
Cover and Text Designer . . . . Stan Green
Illustrator . . . . Laurel Strand
Photographer . . . . Brent Kane

Favorite Christmas Quilts from That Patchwork Place
© 1999 by Martingale & Company

Martingale & Company
PO Box 118
Bothell, WA 98041-0118 USA
www.patchwork.com

That Patchwork Place is an imprint of
Martingale & Company.

Printed in Canada
04 03 02 01 00 99   6 5 4 3 2 1

Library of Congress Cataloging-in-Publication Data is available

⁂ MISSION STATEMENT ⁂
We are dedicated to providing quality products and service by working
together to inspire creativity and to enrich the lives we touch.

Contents

Introduction

4

Quiltmaking Basics

6

Projects

18

Introduction

When it comes to Christmas, quilts have a special way of capturing memories. Whether they're hung on a wall, draped over a chair, admired on a bed, or unpacked each year just for cuddling by the fire, quilts bring warm recollections of holidays past and build new memories for the future.

It's been a special labor of love to put together *Favorite Christmas Quilts from That Patchwork Place* because of the people who were a part of it—our very own staff. We asked our Martingale & Company staff members to choose their favorite quilt designs from our books and transform them into fun holiday quilts, using the latest Christmas fabrics and motifs. What emerged from that request is nothing short of outstanding— fourteen fabulously festive quilt designs, from dramatic traditional bed quilts to short-and-sweet designs to stitch up in a snap.

The quilts created by our talented staff were designed by some of our most popular authors, including Roxanne Carter, Joan Hanson, Little Quilts, Nancy J. Martin, Carolann Palmer, Ursula Reikes, and Margaret Rolfe. You'll find a wide variety of holiday themes, from enchanting ornaments and shimmery snowflakes to traditional holly and berries—we've even got a Santa-style Sunbonnet Sue! A range of quiltmaking techniques are represented, from traditional machine piecing and appliqué to foundation paper piecing and delightful embellishments. The versatility of the designs featured guarantee a project to anyone's liking (even that one person on your gift list who you swear has everything!).

Because the book is based on creating Christmas quilts from patterns not necessarily designed for the holidays, *Favorite Christmas Quilts from That Patchwork Place* also offers a unique opportunity to stretch your quiltmaking imagination. If you are especially drawn to a particular quilt design, try making up the pattern in your favorite non-Christmas colors and fabrics—perhaps pretty pastels for a springtime quilt or fuzzy flannels for a quilt you can use throughout the autumn and winter months. Once you get inspired about the idea of changing colors and fabrics in a design to fit your style and your preferences (like our staff did), you'll start looking at every quilt pattern you see in a whole new way!

So if you're looking for sew-up-quick patterns, precious heirloom designs, or cheery, fun holiday quilts, we've got something for everyone packed into these pages. Stitch up a handmade gift for a special someone, make a unique decorative accent for your holiday home, or create a quilt just for you (if you're like me, you can never have too many). Whether you're adding to or just starting up your stash of quilt memories, we hope these quilts will provide you with memories to last a lifetime.

Mary V. Green

Mary V. Green
Editorial Director

Quiltmaking Basics

Fabric

Select high-quality, 100% cotton fabrics. All-cotton fabrics hold their shape well and are easy to handle. Cotton blends can be more difficult to stitch and press. Sometimes, however, a cotton blend is worth a little extra effort if it is the perfect fabric for your quilt.

Yardage requirements for all the projects in this book are based on 42" of usable fabric after preshrinking. Some quilts call for an assortment of scraps. If you have access to scraps, feel free to use them and purchase only those fabrics you need to complete the quilt you are making.

Preshrink all fabric to test for colorfastness and remove excess dye. Wash dark and light colors separately so that dark colors do not run onto light fabrics. Some fabrics may require several rinses to eliminate the excess dyes. Press the fabric so you can cut out the pieces accurately.

Supplies

Sewing Machine: To machine piece, you'll need a sewing machine that has a good straight stitch. You'll also need a walking foot or darning foot if you are going to machine quilt.

Rotary-Cutting Tools: You will need a rotary cutter, cutting mat, and clear acrylic rulers in a variety of sizes, including 6" x 6", 6" x 24", 12" x 12", and 15" x 15".

Thread: Use a good-quality, all-purpose cotton or cotton-covered polyester thread.

Needles: For machine piecing, a size 70/10 or 80/12 works well for most cottons. For hand appliqué, choose a needle that will glide easily through the edges of the appliqué pieces. Size 10 (fine) to size 12 (very fine) needles work well.

Pins: Long, fine "quilter's" pins with glass or plastic heads are easy to handle. Small ½"- to ¾"-long sequin pins work well for appliqué.

Scissors: Use your best scissors to cut fabric only. Use an older pair of scissors to cut paper, cardboard, and template plastic. Small, 4" scissors are handy for clipping threads.

Sandpaper Board: This is an invaluable tool for accurately marking fabric. You can easily make one by adhering very fine sandpaper to a hard surface, such as wood, cardboard, poster board, or needlework mounting board. The sandpaper grabs the fabric and keeps it from slipping as you mark.

Template Plastic: Use clear or frosted plastic (available at quilt shops) to make durable, accurate templates.

Seam Ripper: Use this tool to remove stitches from incorrectly sewn seams.

Marking Tools: A variety of tools are available to mark fabrics when tracing around templates or marking quilting lines. Use a sharp #2 pencil or fine-lead mechanical pencil on light-colored fabrics; use a silver or yellow marking pencil on dark fabrics. Chalk pencils or chalk-wheel markers also make clear marks on fabric. Be sure to test your marking tool to make sure you can remove its marks easily.

Rotary Cutting

Instructions for quick-and-easy rotary cutting are provided wherever possible. All measurements include standard ¼"-wide seam allowances. For those unfamiliar with rotary cutting, a brief introduction is provided below. For more detailed information, see Donna Thomas's *Shortcuts: A Concise Guide to Rotary Cutting* (That Patchwork Place, 1999).

1. Fold the fabric and match selvages, aligning the crosswise and lengthwise grains as much as possible. Place the folded edge closest to you on the cutting mat. Align a square ruler along the folded edge of the

fabric; then place a long, straight ruler to the left of the square ruler, just covering the uneven raw edges on the left side of the fabric.

Remove the square ruler and cut along the right edge of the long ruler, rolling the rotary cutter away from you. Discard this strip. (Reverse this procedure if you are left-handed.)

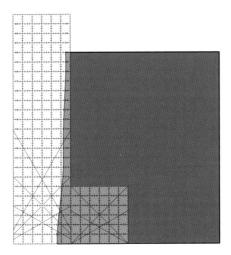

2. To cut strips, align the required measurements on the ruler with the newly cut edge of the fabric. For example, to cut a 2½"-wide strip, place the 2½" ruler mark on the edge of the fabric.

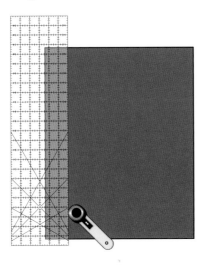

3. To cut squares, cut strips in the required widths. Trim away the selvage ends of the strip. Align the required measurement on the ruler with the left edge of the strip and cut a square. Continue cutting squares until you have the number needed.

Half-Square Triangles

Make half-square triangles by cutting a square in half on the diagonal. The triangle's short sides are on the straight grain of fabric.

1. Cut squares, using the finished measurement of the triangle's short sides, plus ⅞" for seam allowances.
2. Stack squares and cut once diagonally, corner to corner. Each square yields 2 triangles.

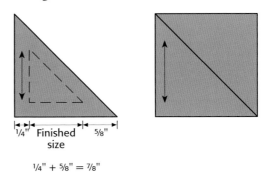

$$\frac{1}{4}'' + \frac{5}{8}'' = \frac{7}{8}''$$

Quarter-Square Triangles

Make quarter-square triangles by cutting a square in quarters on the diagonal. The triangle's long side is on the straight grain of fabric.

1. Cut squares, using the finished measurement of the triangle's long side, plus 1¼" for seam allowances.

2. Stack squares and cut twice diagonally, from corner to corner. Each square yields 4 triangles.

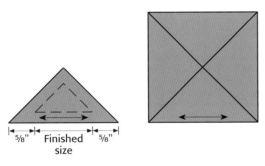

⁵⁄₈" Finished size ⁵⁄₈"

⁵⁄₈" + ⁵⁄₈" = 1 ¼"

Machine Piecing

Making Templates

Most blocks are designed for easy rotary cutting and quick piecing. Some blocks, however, require the use of templates for particular shapes. Templates for machine piecing include the required ¼"-wide seam allowances. Cut out the template on the outside line so it includes the seam allowances. Be sure to mark the pattern name and grain-line arrow on the template.

Sewing Accurate Seam Allowances

The most important thing to remember about machine piecing is to maintain a consistent ¼"-wide seam allowance. Otherwise, the quilt blocks will not be the desired finished size, which in turn affects the size of everything else in the quilt, including alternate blocks, sashings, and borders. Measurements for all components for each quilt are based on blocks that finish accurately to the desired size, plus ¼" on each edge for seam allowances.

Take the time to establish an exact ¼"-wide seam guide on your machine. Some machines have a special foot that measures exactly ¼" from the center needle position to the edge of the foot. This feature allows you

to use the edge of the presser foot to guide the fabric for a perfect ¼"-wide seam allowance.

If your machine doesn't have a such a foot, create a seam guide by placing the edge of a piece of tape or moleskin ¼" from the needle.

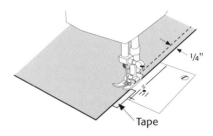

¼"

Tape

Chain Piecing

Chain piecing is an efficient system that saves time.

1. Sew the first pair of pieces from cut edge to cut edge, using 12 stitches per inch. At the end of the seam, stop sewing, but do not cut the thread.

2. Feed the next pair of pieces under the presser foot, as close as possible to the first pair. Continue feeding pieces through the machine without cutting the threads in between. There is no need to backstitch, since each seam will be crossed and held by another seam.

3. When all pieces have been sewn, remove the chain from the machine and clip the threads between the pieces.

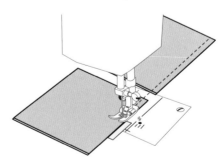

Easing

If two pieces that will be sewn together are slightly different in size (less than ⅛"), pin the places where the two pieces should match and in the middle, if necessary, to distribute the excess fabric evenly. Sew the seam with the longer piece on the bottom. The feed dogs will ease the two pieces together.

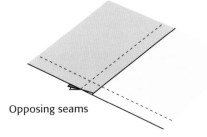

Excess

Pressing

The traditional rule in quiltmaking is to press seams to one side, toward the darker color wherever possible. Press the seam flat from the wrong side first, then press the seam in the desired direction from the right side. Press care-fully to avoid distorting the shapes. Press the seams in the direction of the arrows unless otherwise noted.

When joining two seamed units, plan ahead and press the seam allowances in oppo-site directions as shown to reduce bulk and make it easier to match seam lines. Where two seams meet, the seam allowances will butt against each other, making it easier to join units with perfectly matched seam inter-sections.

Opposing seams

Basic Appliqué

Instructions are provided for needle-turn appliqué. Use another method if you prefer.

Making Templates

Templates made from clear plastic are more durable and accurate than those made from cardboard. Since you can see through the plastic, it is easy to trace the templates accurately.

Place template plastic over each pattern piece and trace with a fine-line permanent marker. Do not add seam allowances. Cut out the templates on the drawn lines. Mark the pattern name and grain-line arrow (if appli-cable) on the template.

Needle-Turn Appliqué

1. Using a plastic template, trace the design onto the right side of the appliqué fabric. Use a #2 pencil on light fabrics, a white or yellow pencil on dark fabrics.
2. Cut out the fabric piece, adding a scant ¼"-wide seam allowance all around.
3. Position the appliqué piece on the back-ground fabric; pin or baste in place.
4. Starting on a straight edge, use the tip of the needle to gently turn under the seam allowance, about ½" at a time. Hold the turned seam allowance firmly between the thumb and first finger of your left hand (reverse if left-handed) as you stitch the appliqué to the background. Use a longer needle—a "sharp" or milliner's needle—to help you control the seam allowance and turn it under neatly. Use the traditional appliqué stitch (page 10) to sew your appliqué pieces to the background.

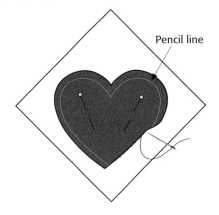

Pencil line

Traditional Appliqué Stitch

The traditional appliqué stitch or blind stitch is appropriate for sewing all appliqué shapes, including sharp points and curves.

1. Tie a knot in a single strand of thread approximately 18" long.
2. Hide the knot by slipping the needle into the seam allowance from the wrong side of the appliqué piece, bringing it out on the fold line.
3. Work from right to left if you are right-handed, or left to right if you are left-handed. Start the first stitch by moving the needle straight off the appliqué, inserting the needle into the background fabric. Let the needle travel under the background fabric, parallel to the edge of the appliqué, bringing it up about ⅛" away, along the pattern line.
4. As you bring the needle up, pierce the edge of the appliqué piece, catching only one or two threads of the folded edge.
5. Move the needle straight off the appliqué into the background fabric. Let your needle travel under the background, bringing it up about ⅛" away, again catching the edge of the appliqué.
6. Give the thread a slight tug and continue stitching.

Appliqué Stitch

7. To end your stitching, pull the needle through to the wrong side. Behind the appliqué piece, take two small stitches, making knots by taking your needle through the loops. Check the right side to see if the thread "shadows" through your background. If it does, take one more small stitch on the back side to direct the tail of the thread under the appliqué fabric.
8. If desired, trim the background fabric that lies under each appliqué piece to reduce the bulk and make it easier to quilt. Turn the block over and make a tiny cut in the background fabric. Trim the fabric ¼" away from the stitching line, being careful not to cut through the appliquéd piece.

Assembling the Quilt Top

Squaring Up Blocks

When your blocks are complete, take the time to square them up. Use a large square ruler to measure your blocks and make sure they are the desired size, plus an extra ¼" on each edge for seam allowances. For example, if you are making 6" blocks, they should all measure 6½" before you sew them together. If your blocks vary slightly in size, trim the larger blocks to match the size of the smallest one. Be sure to trim all four sides; otherwise, your block will be lopsided.

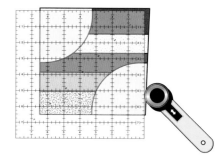

If your blocks are not the required finished size, you will have to adjust all the other components of the quilt accordingly.

Making Straight-Set Quilts

1. Arrange the blocks as shown in the diagram provided with each quilt.
2. Sew blocks together in horizontal rows; press the seams in opposite directions from row to row (unless directed otherwise).

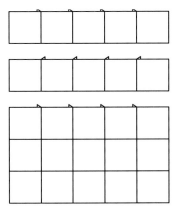

Straight-Set Quilts

3. Sew the rows together, making sure to match the seams between the blocks.

Making Diagonally Set Quilts

1. Arrange the blocks, side triangles, and corner triangles as shown in the diagram provided with each quilt.
2. Sew the blocks together in diagonal rows; press the seams in opposite directions from row to row (unless directed otherwise).
3. Sew the rows together, making sure to match the seams between the blocks. Sew on the corner triangles last.

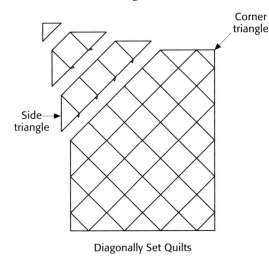

Corner triangle

Side triangle

Diagonally Set Quilts

NOTE: Sometimes side and corner triangles are cut larger than necessary and trimmed later.

Adding Borders

For best results, do not cut border strips and sew them directly to the quilt sides without measuring first. The edges of a quilt often measure slightly longer than the distance through the quilt center, due to stretching during construction. Measure the quilt top through the center in both directions to determine how long to cut the border strips. This step ensures that the finished quilt will be as straight and as "square" as possible, without wavy edges.

Plain borders are commonly cut along the crosswise grain and seamed where extra length is needed. Borders cut from the lengthwise grain of fabric require extra yardage, but seaming to achieve the required length is then unnecessary.

Straight-Cut Borders

1. Measure the length of the quilt top through the center. Cut border strips to that measurement, piecing as necessary. Mark the center of the quilt edges and the border strips. Pin the borders to the sides of the quilt top, matching the center marks and ends and easing as necessary. Sew the border strips in place. Press seams toward the border.

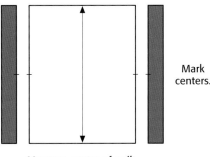

Mark centers.

Measure center of quilt, top to bottom.

2. Measure the width of the quilt top through the center, including the side borders just added. Cut border strips to that measurement, piecing as necessary. Mark the center of the quilt edges and the border strips. Pin the borders to the top and bottom edges of the quilt top, matching the center marks and ends and easing as necessary; stitch. Press seams toward the border.

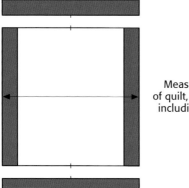

Measure center of quilt, side to side, including borders.

Borders with Corner Squares

1. Measure the width and length of the quilt top through the center. Cut border strips to those measurements, piecing as necessary.

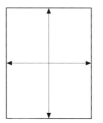

2. Mark the center of the quilt edges and the border strips. Pin the side border strips to opposite sides of the quilt top, matching centers and ends and easing as necessary. Sew the side border strips; press seams toward the border.
3. Cut corner squares the required size (the cut width of the border strips). Sew one corner square to each end of the remaining two border strips; press seams toward the border strips. Pin the border strips to the top and bottom edges of the quilt top.

Match centers, seams between the border strip and corner square, and ends, easing as necessary; stitch. Press seams toward the border.

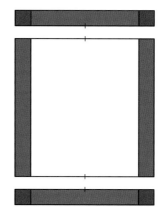

Borders with Mitered Corners

1. First estimate the finished outside dimensions of your quilt, including borders. For example, if your quilt top measures 35½" x 50½" across the center and you want a 5"-wide finished border, your quilt will measure 45" x 60" after the borders are attached. Border strips should be cut to the required measurement, plus at least ½" for seam allowances; it's safer to add 3" to 4" to give yourself some leeway.

NOTE: If your quilt has multiple borders, sew the individual strips together and treat the resulting unit as a single border strip.

2. Fold the quilt in half and mark the center of the quilt edges. Fold each border strip in half and mark the center with a pin.
3. Measure the length and width of the quilt top across the center. Note the measurements.
4. Place a pin at each end of the side border strips to mark the length of the quilt top. Repeat with the top and bottom borders.

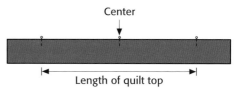

Center

Length of quilt top

5. Pin the borders to the quilt top, matching the centers. Line up the pins at either end of the border strip with the edges of the quilt. Stitch, beginning and ending the stitching ¼" from the raw edges of the quilt top. Repeat with the remaining borders.

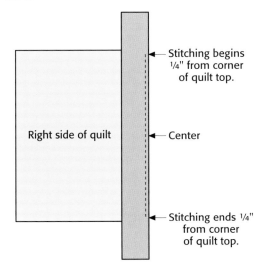

Stitching begins ¼" from corner of quilt top.

Right side of quilt

Center

Stitching ends ¼" from corner of quilt top.

6. Lay the first corner to be mitered on the ironing board. Fold under one border strip at a 45° angle to the other strip. Press and pin.

7. Fold the quilt with right sides together, lining up the edges of the border. If necessary, use a ruler and pencil to draw a line on the crease to make the line more visible. Stitch on the pressed crease, sewing from the corner to the outside edges.

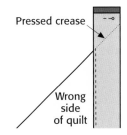

Pressed crease

Wrong side of quilt

8. Press the seam open and trim away excess border strips, leaving a ¼"-wide seam allowance.

9. Repeat with the remaining corners.

Preparing to Quilt

Marking the Quilting Lines

Whether or not to mark the quilting designs depends upon the type of quilting you will be doing. Marking is not necessary if you plan to quilt in-the-ditch, outline-quilt a uniform distance from seam lines, or free-motion quilt in a random pattern. For more complex quilting designs, mark the quilt top before the quilt is layered with batting and backing.

Choose a marking tool that will be visible on your fabric and test it on fabric scraps to be sure the marks can be removed easily. See "Marking Tools" on page 6 for options. Masking tape can also be used to mark straight quilting. Tape only small sections at a time and remove the tape when you stop at the end of the day; otherwise, the sticky residue may be difficult to remove from the fabric.

Layering the Quilt

The quilt "sandwich" consists of the backing, batting, and quilt top. Cut the quilt backing at least 4" larger than the quilt top all the way around. For large quilts, it is usually necessary to sew two or three lengths of fabric together to make a backing the required size. Trim away the selvages before piecing the lengths together. Press the backing seams open to make quilting easier.

Two lengths of fabric seamed in the center

Partial fabric width

Batting comes packaged in standard bed sizes, or it can be purchased by the yard. Several weights or thicknesses are available. Thick battings are fine for tied quilts and comforters; a thinner batting is better, however, if you intend to quilt by hand or machine.

To put it all together:
1. Spread the backing, wrong side up, on a flat, clean surface. Anchor it with pins or masking tape. Be careful not to stretch the backing out of shape.
2. Spread the batting over the backing, smoothing out any wrinkles.
3. Place the pressed quilt top, right side up, on top of the batting. Smooth out any wrinkles and make sure the edges of the quilt top are parallel to the edges of the backing.

4. Starting in the center, baste with needle and thread and work diagonally to each corner. Continue basting in a grid of horizontal and vertical lines 6" to 8" apart. Finish by basting around the edges.

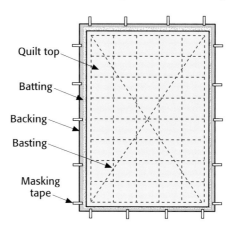

Quilt top
Batting
Backing
Basting
Masking tape

NOTE: For machine quilting, you may baste the layers with #2 rustproof safety pins. Place pins about 6" to 8" apart, away from the area you intend to quilt.

Quilting Techniques

Hand Quilting

To quilt by hand, you will need short, sturdy needles (called "betweens"), quilting thread, and a thimble to fit the middle finger of your sewing hand. Most quilters also use a frame or hoop to support their work. Use the smallest needle you can comfortably handle; the finer the needle, the smaller your stitches will be.
1. Thread your needle with a single strand of quilting thread about 18" long; make a small knot and insert the needle in the top layer about 1" from the place where you want to start stitching. Pull the needle out at the point where quilting will begin and gently pull the thread until the knot pops through the fabric and into the batting.
2. Take small, evenly spaced stitches through all three quilt layers.

3. Rock the needle up and down through all layers, until you have three or four stitches on the needle. Place your other hand underneath the quilt so you can feel the needle point with the tip of your finger when a stitch is taken.

4. To end a line of quilting, make a small knot close to the last stitch; then back-stitch, running the thread a needle's length through the batting. Gently pull the thread until the knot pops into the batting; clip the thread at the quilt's surface.

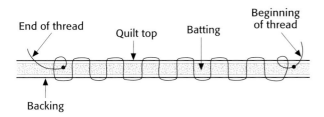

Machine Quilting

Machine quilting is suitable for all types of quilts, from crib to full-size bed quilts. With machine quilting, you can quickly complete quilts that might otherwise languish on the shelves.

For straight-line quilting, it is extremely helpful to have a walking foot to help feed the quilt layers through the machine without shifting or puckering. Some machines have a built-in walking foot; other machines require a separate attachment.

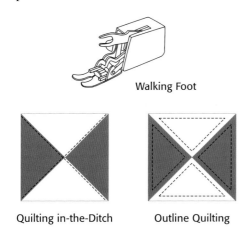

Walking Foot

Quilting in-the-Ditch   Outline Quilting

For free-motion quilting, you need a darning foot and the ability to drop the feed dogs on your machine. With free-motion quilting, you do not turn the fabric under the needle but instead guide the fabric in the direction of the design. Use free-motion quilting to outline-quilt a pattern in the fabric or to create stippling and many other curved designs.

Darning Foot

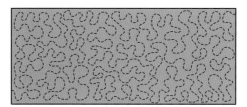

Free-Motion Quilting

Finishing

Binding

For a French double-fold binding, cut strips 2" wide. Cut strips across the width of the fabric. You will need enough strips to go around the perimeter of the quilt, plus 10" for seams and the corners in a mitered fold.

1. Sew strips, right sides together, to make one long piece of binding. Join strips at right angles and stitch across the corner as shown. Trim excess fabric and press the seams open.

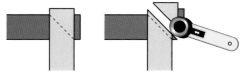

Joining Straight-Cut Strips

2. Fold the strip in half lengthwise, wrong sides together, and press. Turn under ¼" at a 45° angle at one end of the strip and press. Turning the end under at an angle distributes the bulk so you won't have a lump where the two ends of the binding meet.

Fold line

3. Trim the batting and backing even with the quilt top. If you plan to add a sleeve, do so now before attaching the binding (see facing page).

4. Starting on one side of the quilt and using a ¼"-wide seam allowance, stitch the binding to the quilt, keeping the raw edges even with the quilt-top edge. End the stitching ¼" from the corner of the quilt and backstitch. Clip the thread.

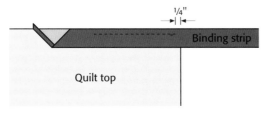
¼"
Binding strip
Quilt top

5. Turn the quilt so that you'll be stitching down the next side. Fold the binding up, away from the quilt, then back down onto itself, parallel with the edge of the quilt top. Begin stitching at the edge, back-stitching to secure. Repeat on the remaining edges and corners of the quilt.

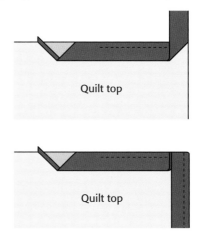
Quilt top

Quilt top

6. When you reach the beginning of the binding, overlap the beginning stitches by about 1" and cut away any excess binding, trimming the end at a 45° angle. Tuck the end of the binding into the fold and finish the seam.

Quilt top

7. Fold the binding over the raw edges of the quilt to the back, with the folded edge covering the row of machine stitching, and blindstitch in place. A miter will form at each corner. Blindstitch the mitered corners.

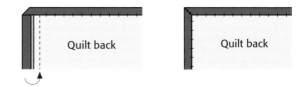
Quilt back   Quilt back

Adding a Sleeve

If you plan to display your finished quilt on the wall, be sure to add a hanging sleeve to hold the rod.

1. Using leftover fabric from the front or a piece of muslin, cut a strip 6" to 8" wide and 1" shorter than the width of the quilt at the top edge. Fold the ends under ½", then ½" again; stitch.

2. Fold the fabric strip in half lengthwise, wrong sides together, and baste the raw edges to the top edge of the quilt back. The top edge of the sleeve will be secured when the binding is sewn on the quilt.

Baste sleeve to top edge of quilt.

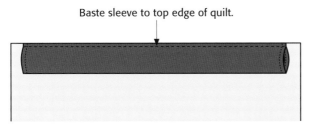

3. Finish the sleeve after the binding has been attached by blindstitching the bottom of the sleeve in place. Push the bottom edge of the sleeve up just a bit to provide a little give so the hanging rod does not put strain on the quilt itself.

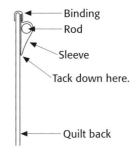

Signing Your Quilt

Future generations will want to know more than just who made your quilt and when. Labels can be as elaborate or as simple as you desire. You can write, type, or embroider the information. Be sure to include your name, the name of the quilt, your city and state, the date, the name of the recipient if it is a gift, and any other interesting or important information about the quilt.

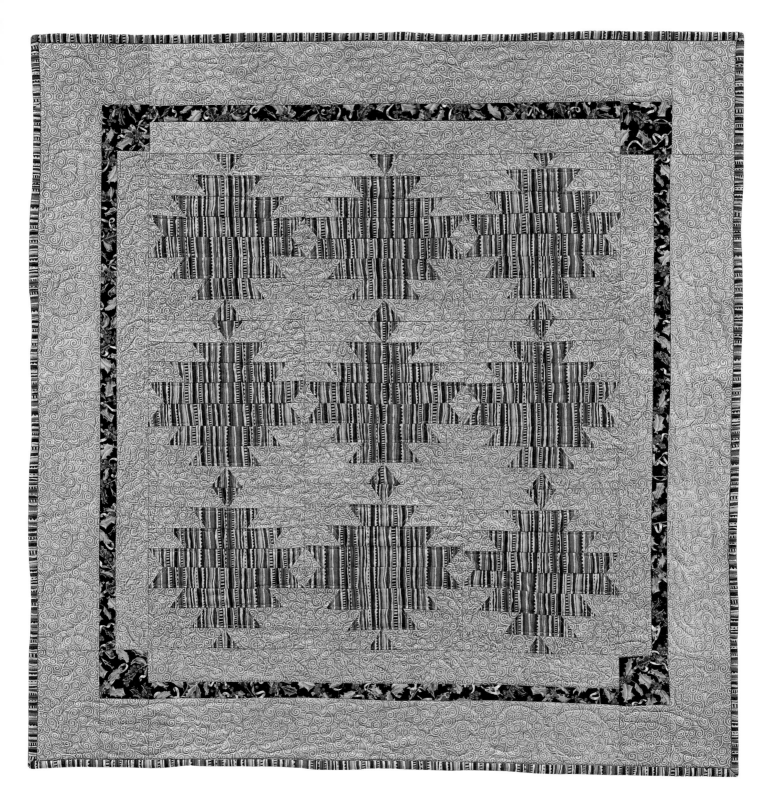

High-Voltage Holiday *by Tamara Peterson, 1999, Woodinville, Washington, 45 ¼" x 45 ¼".*

High-Voltage Holiday

Contemporary squiggles and stripes bring a vibrant energy to this fun quilt by Tamara Peterson.
The pattern, "Momijigari," is taken from Takae Onoyama's *Honoring the Seasons*.
Tamara is a Credit Clerk in our Customer Service Department.

Finished Quilt Size: 45¼" x 45¼"
Finished Block Size: 10¼"

MATERIALS: 44"-wide fabric

- 2¼ yds. green print for background and inner and outer borders
- 1¼ yds. red/green stripe for blocks and binding
- ⅓ yd. dark print for middle border and corner squares
- 3 yds. for backing

Cutting

Cut all strips across the width of the fabric unless otherwise noted. Use the templates on page 21.

From the green print, cut border strips from the lengthwise grain:
- 4 strips, 2½" x 31¼", for inner border
- 2 strips, 4½" x 37¼", for outer side border
- 2 strips, 4½" x 45¼", for outer top and bottom border
- 18 of triangle B
- 18 of triangle B reversed

From the red/green stripe, cut:
- 18 of triangle A
- 5 strips, 2" x 42", for binding

From the dark print, cut:
- 4 strips, 1½" x 31¼", for middle border
- 4 squares, 3½" x 3½", for corner squares

Block Assembly

1. Sew a triangle B and a triangle B reversed to each short side of triangle A.

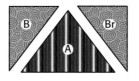 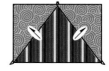

Make 18.

2. Beginning at the long unsewn edge of triangle A, cut across the unit to make 4 pieced strips, 1¾" wide.

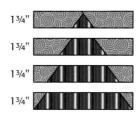

3. Without changing the order of the strips, rotate each piece 180°, then sew the strips together to make a half-block.

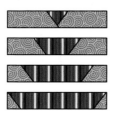 

Make 18.

4. Join the half-blocks to make the block.

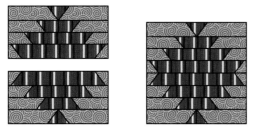

Make 9.

Quilt Assembly and Finishing

1. Arrange the blocks in 3 rows of 3 blocks each. Sew the blocks into horizontal rows. Join the rows.

2. Sew the inner and middle border strips together in pairs.

Make 4.

3. Referring to "Borders with Corner Squares" on page 12, sew a pieced border strip to opposite sides of the quilt top. Add a corner square to the remaining pieced borders and add these to the top and bottom edges.

4. Referring to "Straight-Cut Borders" on pages 11–12, measure, trim, and sew the outer border strips to the side edges of the quilt top first, then to the top and bottom edges.
5. Layer the quilt top with batting and backing; baste. Quilt as desired.
6. Bind the edges and add a label.

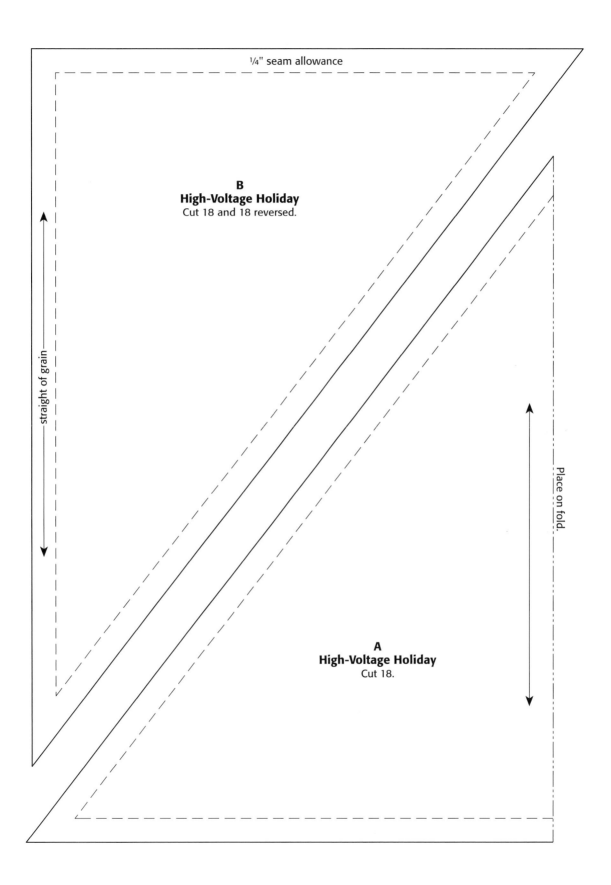

¼" seam allowance

B
High-Voltage Holiday
Cut 18 and 18 reversed.

straight of grain

Place on fold.

A
High-Voltage Holiday
Cut 18.

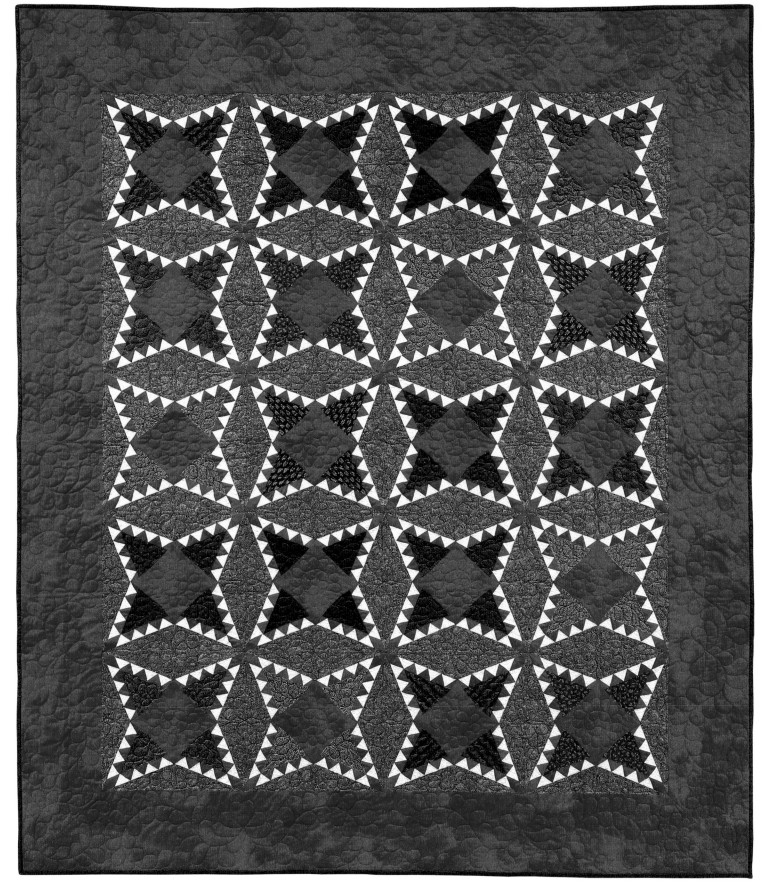

World of Christmas Joy *by Beth Kovich, 1999, Woodinville, Washington, 72 ½" x 86 ½". Machine quilted by Judy Allen.*

World of Christmas Joy

Sales Representative Beth Kovich used paper piecing to create this stunning, heirloom-quality bed quilt, already a family Christmas treasure. The pattern, "Feathered World without End," is from *Classic Quilts with Precise Foundation Piecing* by Tricia Lund and Judy Pollard.

Finished Quilt Size: 72½" x 86½"
Finished Block Size: 14"

MATERIALS: 44"-WIDE FABRIC

6 yds. red print for blocks and border
3 yds. white tone-on-tone print for small triangles
¼ yd. each of 10 assorted green prints for large triangles
2⅞ yds. red/green print for background
5¼ yds. for backing
½ yd. green print for binding
160 sheets of lightweight paper or paper designed for foundation piecing

Cutting

Cut strips across the width of the fabric unless otherwise noted. Use the templates on pages 27–29.

From the red print, cut from the lengthwise grain:
2 strips, 8½" x 75", for side borders
2 strips, 8½" x 90, for top and bottom borders

From the red print, cut from the crosswise grain:
50 strips, 2" x 42"
20 of Template 2

From the white tone-on-tone print, cut:
52 strips, 2" x 42"

From *each* of the 10 green prints, cut:
8 of Template 1 (80 total)

From the red/green print, cut:
80 of Template 3

From the green print for binding, cut:
8 strips, 2" x 42"

Sewing the Foundations

Keep the following points in mind when foundation piecing.

• The unit you place under the presser foot consists of 3 layers: the paper pattern (with the marked side up) on top and 2 layers of fabric, right sides together, beneath the paper. Sew on the seam lines marked on the paper. Trim the seam allowance to ¼". Stitch the seams in consecutive order: the seam between fabrics 1 and 2, then the seam between 2 and 3, and so on until the foundation is complete.

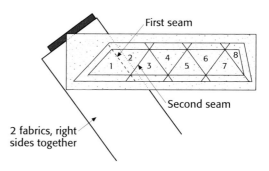

• After you sew a piece and open it, check to make sure the fabric covers its allotted place, with enough extra for the seam allowance on the next seam.

• When the foundation is complete, trim along the outside cutting line.

• Use 15 to 18 stitches per inch to make paper removal easier. If you do make a mistake and need to redo a seam, just put a piece of tape over the perforated seam on the marked side of the paper.

• Do not remove the paper foundation until you are ready to sew the units into blocks. This helps prevent the distortion that can be caused by handling.

• Remember, the finished unit is a mirror image of the foundation.

Constructing the Teeth Units

1. Place fabrics 1 and 2 right sides together. With the marked side of the paper up, place the fabrics beneath position 1, with piece 1 against the paper. Make sure the fabrics are large enough to cover the spaces, including seam allowances.

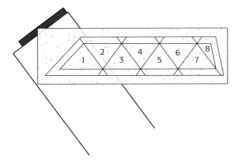

2. Hold the fabrics in position and place the unit under the presser foot, paper side up. Sew along the line between positions 1 and 2, through the paper and both layers of fabric.

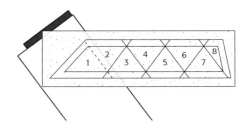

3. Trim the seam allowance to ¼".
4. Fold back piece 2 and press. Trim the excess strips just beyond the foundation.

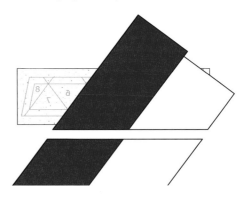

5. Place a strip of fabric for piece 3 right sides together with fabric 2. Make sure the fabric is large enough to cover position 3, including seam allowances.

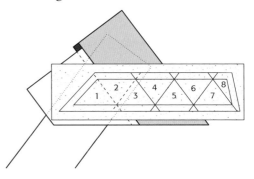

6. Sew along the stitching line. Trim the seam allowance to ¼", fold back, and press. Continue piecing until the unit is complete.

7. Trim along the outside cutting line.

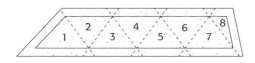

8. Do not remove the paper yet.

Block Assembly

1. Make 80 photocopies each of foundation 1 and foundation 2 on pages 27 and 29.

2. Referring to the directions on the facing page, construct 80 foundation 1. Use the white in position 1 and the red in position 2, then alternate white and red.

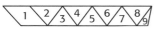

Foundation 1

Make 80.

3. Make 80 foundation 2. Use red for position 1 (diamond) and white for position 2. Alternate red and white.

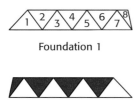

Foundation 2

Make 80.

4. Arrange 2 teeth units with a triangle (Template 1) and sew them together. Be sure the bases of the white teeth are on the outside edge of the unit.

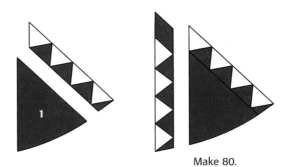

Make 80.

5. Arrange 4 units with identical triangle fabrics (Template 1) around a center piece (Template 2). Pin the seams, then sew them together, beginning and ending your stitching ¼" from the end of the seam. Remove the paper foundations.

Begin and end stitching ¼" from edge.

6. Add the red/green background pieces (Template 3). Begin stitching at the ¼" mark, then backstitch, and sew to the outside edge. Repeat on the other edge of the triangle.

Stitch from center mark to edge.

Stitch from center mark to edge.

Make 20.

Quilt Assembly and Finishing

1. Arrange the blocks in 5 rows of 4 blocks each. Sew the blocks together in horizontal rows. Join the rows.

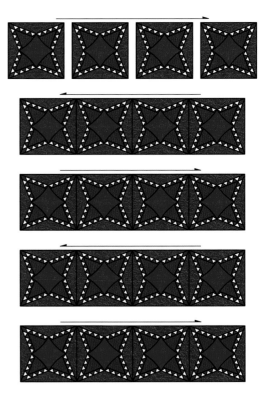

2. Referring to "Borders with Mitered Corners" on pages 12–13, sew the border strips to the quilt top, mitering the corners.
3. Layer the quilt top with batting and backing; baste. Quilt as desired.
4. Bind the edges and add a label.

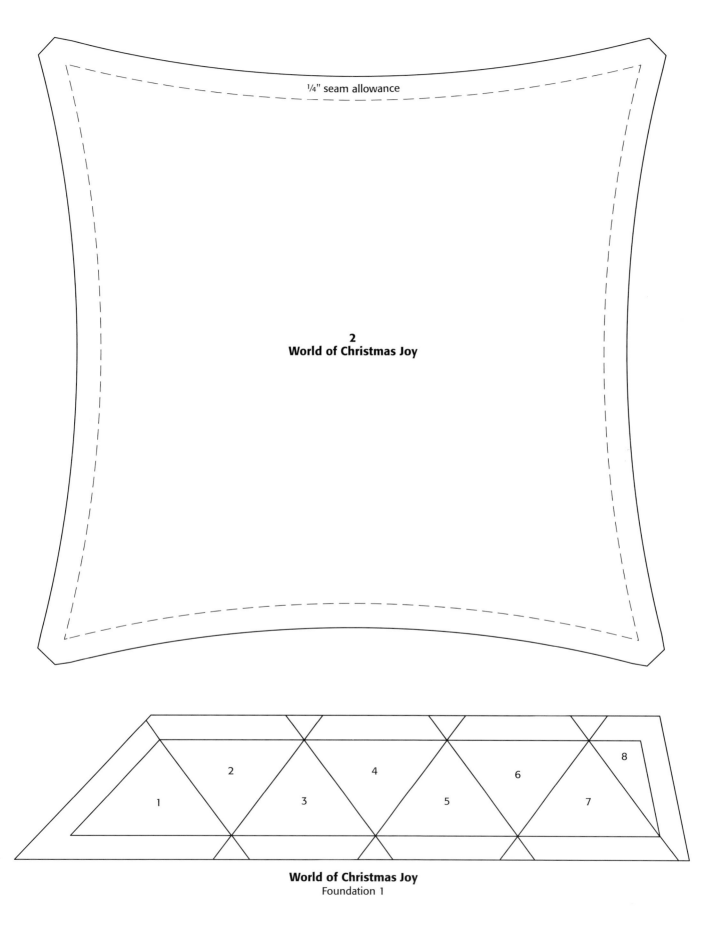

¼" seam allowance

2
World of Christmas Joy

| 2 | | 4 | | 6 | | 8 |
| 1 | 3 | | 5 | | 7 | |

World of Christmas Joy
Foundation 1

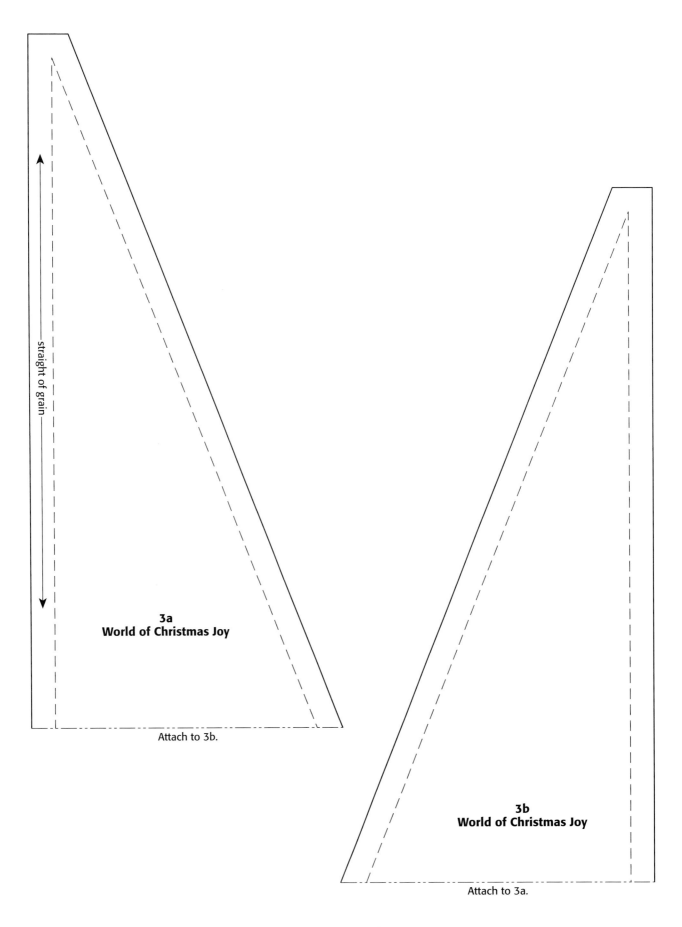

straight of grain

3a
World of Christmas Joy

Attach to 3b.

3b
World of Christmas Joy

Attach to 3a.

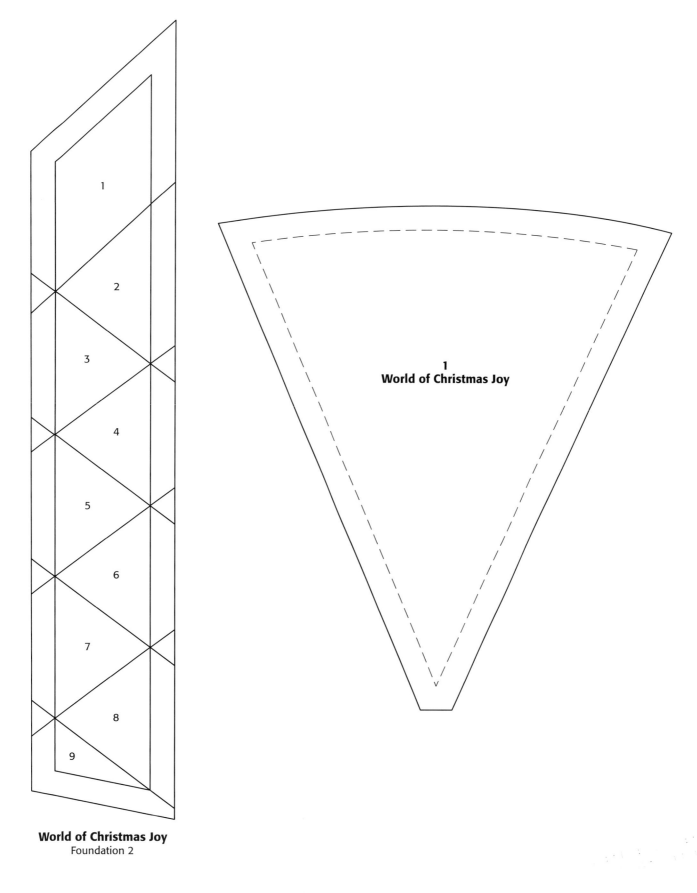

**1
World of Christmas Joy**

World of Christmas Joy
Foundation 2

Jolly Holly Balls *by Tamara Peterson, 1999, Woodinville, Washington, 39½" x 51½".*

Jolly Holly Balls

Glittering gold lamé and rich red ribbons become sparkling holiday ornaments in this wall quilt by Tamara Peterson. The pattern, "Beach Balls," was originally published in *Calendar Quilts* by Joan Hanson.

Finished Quilt Size: 39½" x 51½"
Finished Block Size: 6"

MATERIALS: 44"-wide fabric

- ⅛ yd. each of 30 assorted Christmas prints for blocks
- 1 yd. gold tissue lamé for balls
- 1½ yds. fusible knit interfacing
- ⅝ yd. red solid for inner border and binding
- ⅝ yd. green solid for outer border
- 1⅝ yds. for backing
- 4¾ yds. large gold rickrack for border trim (optional)
- 3 yds. of 2"-wide red/gold wire-edge ribbon for bows (optional)

Cutting

Cut strips across the width of the fabric.

From *each* of the 30 Christmas prints, cut:
1 strip, 1¹¹⁄₁₆" wide. You will need to cut between the 1⅝" and 1¾" marks on your acrylic ruler. Put a piece of masking tape on the ruler to help you find the place for each cut.

From the gold tissue lamé*, cut:
12 circles, 7" in diameter. Use Template B on page 35 to cut them into quarters.

From the red solid, cut:
4 strips, 2" x 42", for inner border
5 strips, 2" x 42", for binding

From the green solid, cut:
5 strips, 3½" x 42", for outer border

*Iron fusible knit interfacing (following manufacturer's instructions) to the wrong side of the gold tissue lamé before cutting circles.

Block Assembly

1. Divide the Christmas prints into 6 groups of 5 prints each. Sew each group of strips together to make 6 strip sets. The strip sets should measure 6½" wide. Check the first one and adjust your seam allowance if you are off. From each strip set, cut 4 squares, 6½" x 6½".

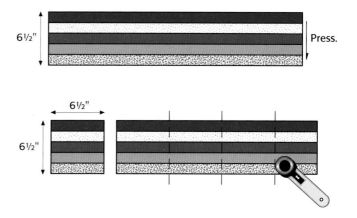

2. Using Template A on page 35, cut a quarter-circle off 2 opposite corners of each square.

NOTE: Be sure to work with the right side of the block facing up and line up the dashed lines on the template with the strip seams, or your blocks will be backward.

3. Sew 2 gold quarter-circles (B) to each striped piece to make the block. Curved seams may be sewn by hand or machine. The technique is basically the same using either method.

4. Locate the center of each curved seam by folding the fabric in half. Pin the solid quarter-circle and the striped piece together at the centers. Pin through the seam allowances at each end.

Center of curve

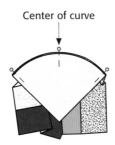

5. Gently stretch the inner curve (the striped piece) to fit it to the outer curve (the solid piece). Add more pins as needed. You can make a few clips into the inner-curve seam allowance.

Clip as needed.

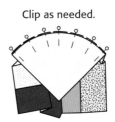

6. Start stitching by hand or machine at the center pin and sew out to the end. Start again at the center and sew out to the other end.

Start stitching here.

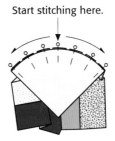

If you are sewing by hand, do not knot your thread, but leave a 6" tail when you stitch from the center to the other end. Rethread this tail to complete the seam to the other end.

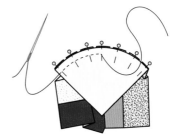

7. Sew on all the cut-out curves. Press the seams toward the quarter-circles.

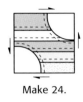

Make 24.

Quilt Assembly and Finishing

1. Arrange the blocks in 6 rows of 4 blocks each as shown. Sew the blocks together in horizontal rows.

2. Join the rows.
3. Referring to "Straight-Cut Borders" on pages 11–12, measure, trim, and sew the inner border strips to the side edges of the quilt top, then to the top and bottom edges.

4. From each of the leftover strip sets, cut 4 segments, 3½" wide.

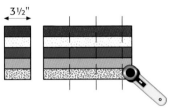

3½"

5. Sew the segments together to make middle border strips long enough to fit the 4 sides of your quilt. The top and bottom strips are the width of your quilt to this point (including seam allowances), plus one finished width of your border; 27½" + 3" = 30½". The sides are the length of your quilt to this point (including seam allowances), plus one finished width of your border; 39½" + 3" = 42½".
6. Starting in the upper left corner, sew on the pieced border strip. Stop stitching 2" from the end.

Start here.

Stop 2" from the end.

7. Add a pieced border to the left side.

8. Add a pieced border to the bottom, then to the right side. Finish the seam, attaching the top pieced border.

← Finish stitching this seam.

9. Sew the outer border strips to the quilt top as for the inner border.
10. Layer the quilt with batting and backing; baste. Quilt as desired.
11. Bind the edges and add a label.
12. *Optional:* Machine stitch large gold rick-rack between the middle pieced and outer borders, using transparent nylon thread. Cut the red/gold wire-edge ribbon into 1-yard lengths, tie each length into a bow, and sew by hand to the quilt.

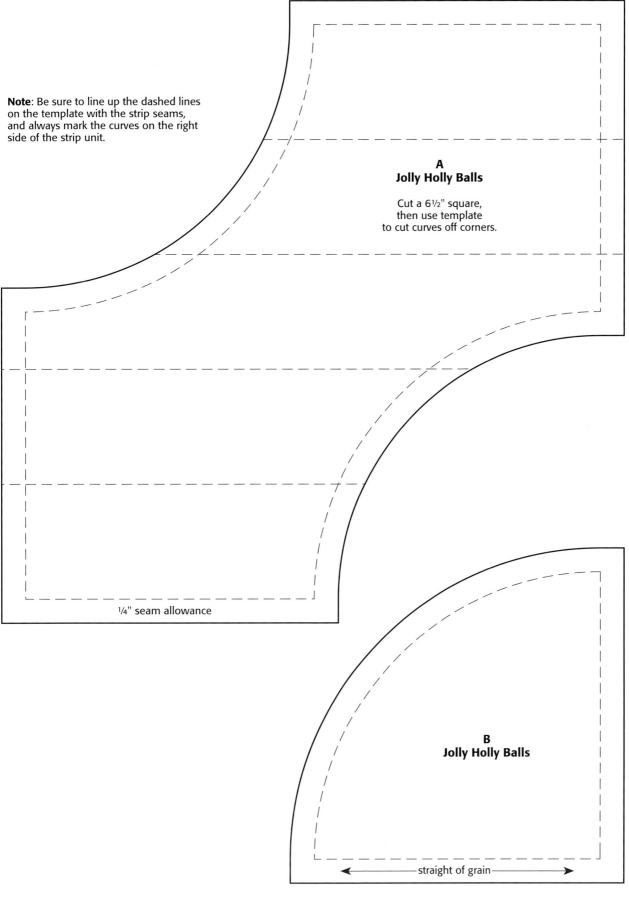

Note: Be sure to line up the dashed lines on the template with the strip seams, and always mark the curves on the right side of the strip unit.

A
Jolly Holly Balls

Cut a 6½" square, then use template to cut curves off corners.

¼" seam allowance

B
Jolly Holly Balls

←————— straight of grain —————→

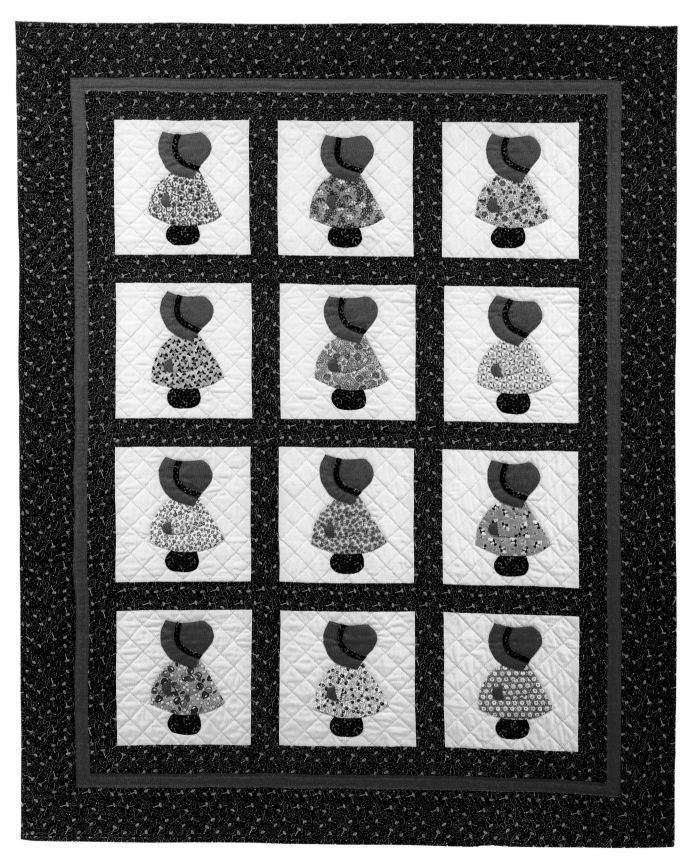

Sue's Christmas Best *by Beth Kovich and Molly Merrill, 1999, Woodinville, Washington, 58" x 72½".*
Hand quilted by Laura Raber.

Sue's Christmas Best

Beth Kovich dressed up the ever-popular Sunbonnet Sue in holiday style, using her stash of '30s reproduction fabrics. Molly Merrill, Beth's mother, provided the beautiful hand appliqué. The design was inspired by a Sue block from *Pieces of the Past* by Nancy J. Martin.

Finished Quilt Size: 58" x 72½"
Finished Block Size: 12"

MATERIALS: 44"-wide fabric

1½ yds. muslin for background

⅜ yd. bright red solid for Sue's hat and mitten

⅛ yd. black print for Sue's shoe and hatband

8" x 8" square of 12 different prints for Sue's dress

2⅜ yds. green print for sashing, inner and outer borders, and binding

½ yd. red solid for middle border

4½ yds. for backing

Cutting

Cut strips across the width of the fabric. Use the templates on page 39.

From the muslin, cut:
4 strips, 13" x 42"; crosscut the strips into 12 squares, 13" x 13". They will be trimmed to 12½" after the appliqué is complete.

From the bright red solid, cut:
12 of Template 3 (mitten)
12 of Template 5 (hat)

From the black print, cut:
12 bias strips, each 1½" x 5½" for hatband
12 of Template 1 (shoe)

From *each* dress print, cut:
1 of Template 2 (dress)
1 of Template 4 (sleeve)

From the green print, cut:
3 strips, 3" x 42"; crosscut the strips into 8 rectangles, 3" x 12½", for vertical sashing
3 strips, 3" x 41½", for horizontal sashing
5 strips, 3" x 42", for inner border
6 strips, 5" x 42", for outer border
7 strips, 2" x 42", for binding

From the red solid, cut:
6 strips, 1¾" x 42", for middle border

Block Assembly

1. Fold a black bias strip in half, wrong sides together, and stitch ⅛" from the raw edges.

2. Press the tube so the seam falls in the middle of the back. Make 12.

3. Appliqué a bias tube on each hat (Template 5).

4. Arrange the appliqué pieces on the background square; pin or baste in place. Appliqué Sue in numerical order. Refer to "Basic Appliqué" on page 9.

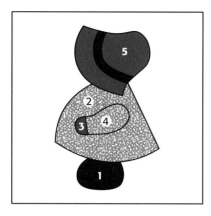

5. Trim the background square to 12½" x 12½". Be sure to trim from all four sides; otherwise, your block will be lopsided.

Quilt Assembly and Finishing

1. Sew 3 blocks and 2 vertical sashing strips together to make each of 4 rows. Press the seams toward the sashing.

Make 4.

2. Join the rows, adding the horizontal sashing strips between them. Press the seams toward the sashing.

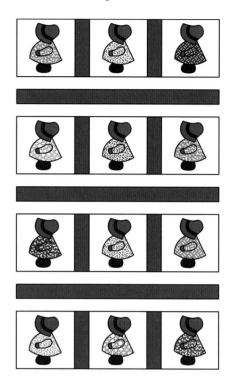

3. Referring to "Straight-Cut Borders" on pages 11–12, measure, trim, and sew the inner border strips to the side edges of the quilt top first, then to the top and bottom edges. Repeat for the middle and outer borders.
4. Layer the quilt with batting and backing; baste. Quilt as desired.
5. Bind the edges and add a label.

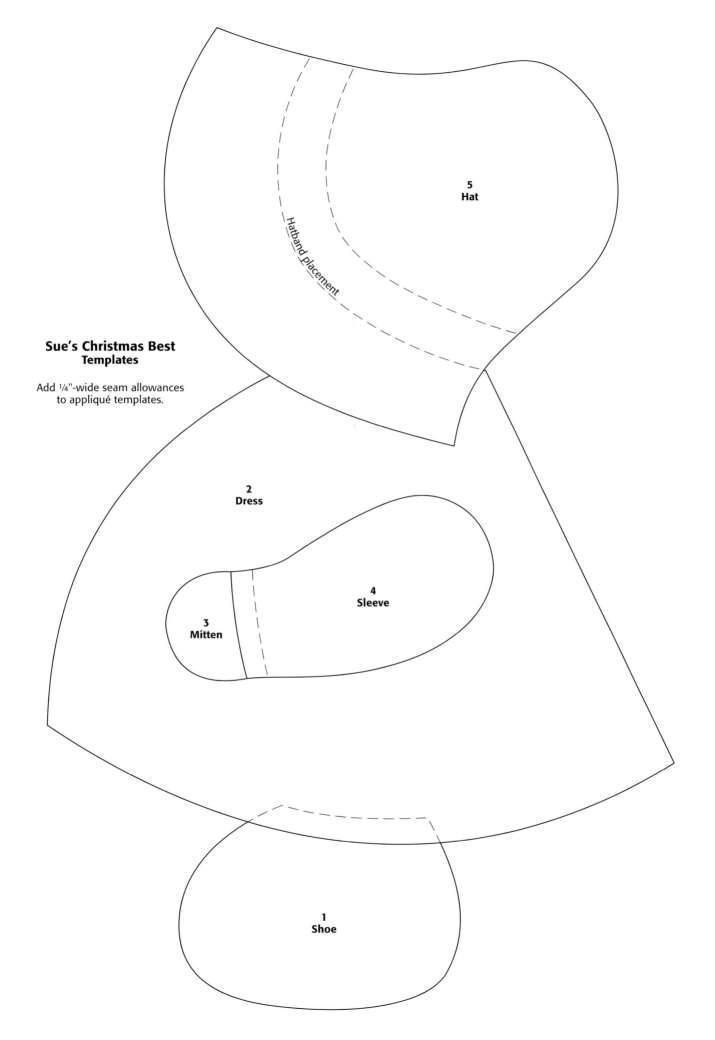

Sue's Christmas Best
Templates

Add ¼"-wide seam allowances
to appliqué templates.

5
Hat

Hatband placement

2
Dress

4
Sleeve

3
Mitten

1
Shoe

Snow and Ice *by Rhoda Lonergan, 1999, Monroe, Washington, 56⅛" x 56⅛".*

Snow and Ice

Crisp blue and silvery gray fabrics bring to mind a chilly winter evening in this quilt by Customer Service Representative Rhoda Lonergan. Billowy snowflakes, hand quilted in shimmery metallic thread, add to its wintry appeal. The pattern, "Rolling Pinwheel," comes from *101 Fabulous Rotary-Cut Quilts* by Nancy J. Martin and Judy Hopkins.

Finished Quilt Size: 56⅛" x 56⅛"
Finished Block Size: 9"

MATERIALS: 44"-wide fabric

2 yds. white tone-on-tone print for background
⅞ yd. gray/white print for blocks and binding
⅜ yd. dark print for inner border
1⅛ yds. floral print for outer border
3½ yds. for backing

Cutting

Cut strips across the width of the fabric.

From the white tone-on-tone print, cut:

2 strips, 2" x 42"; crosscut strips into 36 squares, 2" x 2".
3 strips, 2⅜" x 42"; crosscut strips into 36 squares, 2⅜" x 2⅜". Cut squares once diagonally to yield 72 half-square triangles.
1 strip, 4¼" x 42"; crosscut strip into 9 squares, 4¼" x 4¼". Cut squares twice diagonally to yield 36 quarter-square triangles.

2 strips, 7¼" x 42"; crosscut strips into 36 rectangles, 2" x 7¼". Trim the corners of the rectangles at a 45° angle.

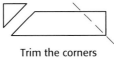

Trim the corners at a 45° angle.

1 strip, 9½" x 42"; crosscut strip into 4 squares, 9½" x 9½", for alternate blocks.
1 strip, 19" x 42"; crosscut strip into 2 squares, 19" x 19". Cut squares twice diagonally to yield 8 quarter-square triangles for side triangles. These are cut extra large to allow the blocks to "float."
2 squares, 11¾" x 11¾". Cut squares once diagonally to yield 4 half-square triangles for corner triangles. These pieces are also cut extra large.

From the gray/white print, cut:
   5 strips, 2⅜" x 42"; crosscut strips into 72 squares, 2⅜" x 2⅜". Cut squares once diagonally to yield 144 half-square triangles.
   1 strip, 4¼" x 42"; crosscut strip into 9 squares, 4¼" x 4¼". Cut squares twice diagonally to yield 36 quarter-square triangles.
   7 strips, 2" x 42, for binding

From the dark print, cut:
   5 strips, 2" x 42", for inner border

From the floral print, cut:
   6 strips, 6" x 42", for outer border

Block Assembly

1. Join two 2⅜" white half-square triangles and a gray/white 4¼" quarter-square triangle. Join two 2⅜" gray/white half-square triangles and a white 4¼" quarter-square triangle.

Make 36.   Make 36.

2. Join the units you made in step 1.

Make 36.

3. Join 2 gray/white half-square triangles to the ends of a trimmed white rectangle.

Make 36.

4. Piece a Rolling Pinwheel block as shown.

Rolling Pinwheel
Make 9.

Quilt Assembly and Finishing

1. Arrange and sew the Rolling Pinwheel blocks, alternate blocks, and side and corner triangles in diagonal rows. Join the rows, adding the corner triangles last. Trim the outside edges and square up the corners of the quilt as necessary, leaving 2" of fabric outside the block corners to allow the blocks to float.

2. Referring to "Straight-Cut Borders" on pages 11–12, measure, trim, and sew the inner border strips to the side edges of the quilt top first, then to the top and bottom edges. Repeat for the outer border.

3. Layer with batting and backing; quilt or tie. Quilt as desired.

4. Bind the edges and add a label.

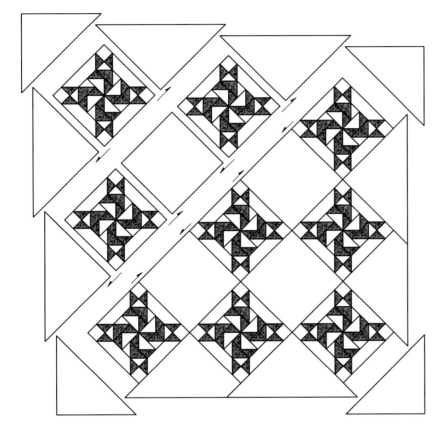

Roses and Wreaths *by Virginia Lauth, 1999, Shoreline, Washington, 59½" x 75½".*

Roses and Wreaths

Traditional red-and-green Old Favorite blocks drift on a snowy-white background in this quilt by Virginia Lauth, Accounts Manager. Virginia's hand quilting accents this simple-to-stitch design. The pattern is "Northern Nites" from *Two-Color Quilts* by Nancy J. Martin.

Finished Quilt Size: 59½" x 75½"

NOTE: This quilt is constructed in units as a bar quilt. The units are joined into rows rather than blocks.

MATERIALS: 44"-wide fabric

2⅞ yds. white tone-on-tone print for units and inner border

1⅞ yds. green tone-on-tone print for units, outer border, and binding

1⅛ yds. red tone-on-tone print for units and middle border

4⅝ yds. fabric for backing

Cutting

Cut strips across the width of the fabric.

NOTE: Keep the half- and quarter-square triangles separate to avoid confusion.

From the white tone-on-tone print, cut:
13 strips, 4½" x 42"; crosscut 2 strips into 28 rectangles, 2½" x 4½". Crosscut remaining strips into 82 squares, 4½" x 4½".

5 strips, 2⅞" x 42"; crosscut strips into 62 squares, 2⅞" x 2⅞". Cut squares once diagonally to yield 124 half-square triangles.

2 strips, 5¼" x 42"; crosscut strips into 9 squares, 5¼" x 5¼". Cut squares twice diagonally to yield 36 quarter-square triangles. You will use 34 and have 2 left over.

6 strips, 2" x 42", for inner border

From the green tone-on-tone print, cut:
3 strips, 4⅞" x 42"; crosscut strips into 24 squares, 4⅞" x 4⅞". Cut squares once diagonally to yield 48 half-square triangles.

2 strips, 5¼" x 42"; crosscut strips into 12 squares, 5¼" x 5¼". Cut squares twice diagonally to yield 48 quarter-square triangles.

7 strips, 3" x 42", for outer border

7 strips, 2" x 42", for binding

From the red tone-on-tone print, cut:
3 strips, 4½" x 42"; crosscut strips into 18 squares, 4½" x 4½", and 10 rectangles, 2½" x 4½"

4 strips, 2½" x 42"; crosscut strips into 52 squares, 2½" x 2½"

6 strips, 2" x 42", for middle border

Unit and Row Assembly

1. Join 2 white half-square triangles and a green quarter-square triangle to make Unit A.

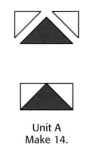

Unit A
Make 14.

2. Join 2 white half-square triangles, 1 red 2½" square, and 1 green half-square triangle to make Unit B.

Unit B
Make 48.

3. Join 2 green quarter-square triangles and 2 white quarter-square triangles to make Unit C.

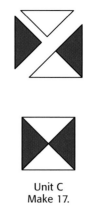

Unit C
Make 17.

4. Join 2 red 2½" squares, 2 red rectangles, 6 white rectangles, and 3 of Unit A to make Row A.

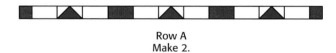

Row A
Make 2.

5. Join 5 white 4½" squares, 2 white rectangles, and 6 of Unit B to make Row B.

Row B
Make 8.

6. Join 6 white 4½" squares, 3 red 4½" squares, 2 of Unit A, and 2 of Unit C to make Row C.

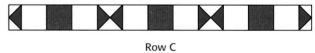

Row C
Make 4.

7. Join 6 white 4½" squares, 2 red 4½" squares, 2 red rectangles, and 3 of Unit C to make Row D.

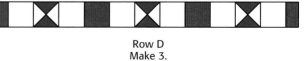

Row D
Make 3.

Quilt Assembly and Finishing

1. Join the rows. Rows marked * are turned upside down.

2. Referring to "Straight-Cut Borders" on pages 11–12, measure, trim, and sew the inner border strips to the side edges of the quilt top first, then to the top and bottom edges. Repeat for the middle and outer borders.
3. Layer the quilt top with batting and backing. Quilt as desired.
4. Bind the edges and add a label.

A Very Beary Christmas

Mama, Papa, and Baby Bear—the Polar variety—frolic through a star-filled night in this delightful wall quilt by Marketing Graphic Designer Julia Kartawidjaja. The Black Bear and Tree blocks are from *Go Wild with Quilts* by Margaret Rolfe.

Finished Quilt Size: 47" x 21½"

A Very Beary Christmas by Julia Kartawidjaja, 1999, Woodinville, Washington, 47" x 21½".

MATERIALS: 44"-wide fabric

½ yd. blue/white print for outer border
½ yd. navy blue print for background
½ yd. green print for trees and inner border
¼ yd. white tone-on-tone print for bears
Scrap of off-white for bear muzzles
Scrap of brown for tree trunks
1½ yds. for backing
¼ yd. navy blue/white print for binding

Assorted star buttons for trees and sky
3 tiny buttons for bear eyes
6" of 1"-wide ribbon for Papa Bear tie
2 small pompons for Baby and Mama Bear earmuffs

NOTE: Before beginning this quilt, read through the following directions for making the Bear and Tree blocks, which are pieced using Margaret Rolfe's straight-line patchwork technique.

Piecing the Blocks

The blocks are easy to sew because all pieces are sewn together with straight seams, thus the name, straight-line patchwork. The concept behind straight-line patchwork is simple, and like any technique, it has its own rules.

Rule Number 1. Follow the piecing order. Each block is numbered.

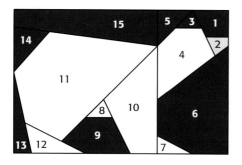

The plus sign always indicates a seam. When the piecing order says 1 + 2, pick up pieces 1 and 2 and sew them together. Once joined, the pieces become a unit, which is signified by putting the numbers into parentheses and placing a dash between the numbers.

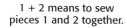

1 + 2 means to sew pieces 1 and 2 together.

Once sewn, the pieces are a unit called (1–2).

The piecing order is given as a series of lettered steps, which look like this:

A. 1+ 2
B. 3 + 4
C. (1–2) + (3– 4) + 5

These are the first three steps in putting the Bear block together. You have now created a unit, which in the next step will be called (1–5) because it comprises all the pieces from 1 through 5.

Each step is lettered so you know exactly where you are and represents a seam (or number of seams) that can be sewn without crossing another seam. Following the piecing order is much like following a knitting pattern; you knit rows in the correct order: you don't knit row 5 before row 3.

In straight-line patchwork, pieces are sewn together into units that may be temporarily set aside while another unit is being sewn. Completed units are then sewn together into a larger unit or section.

Rule Number 2. Lay out the block, with each piece in its correct position, before you begin to sew. This will help you determine which sides of the pieces should be sewn together.

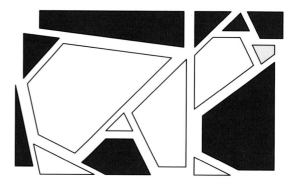

Rule Number 3. Mark seam lines and do not automatically add seam allowances. There is a good reason for this, which you will discover when you actually sew two pieces together. The odd shapes in straight-line patchwork do not sit neatly on top of each other, with corners accurately matched like two squares or two identical triangles do. Seam lines are marked so that pieces will match up correctly at the corners. In fact, it is similar to the procedure for hand piecing except the sewing can be done by machine.

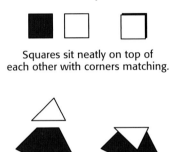

Squares sit neatly on top of each other with corners matching.

The odd shapes in straight-line patchwork will not match at the corners unless seam lines are marked.

Rule Number 4. Use ⅜" to ½" seam allowances, adding them as you cut around the marked shapes. I suggest cutting a ⅜"-wide seam allowance on most pieces and a full ½"-wide seam allowance on small and long, pointed pieces. The wide seam allowances give you more fabric with which to pin and stitch, and the pieces are less likely to move as you sew. Do not mark a ¼" cutting line outside your marked seam line. This adds an unnecessary, time-consuming step. Trim excess fabric from the wider seam allowances after the seam is sewn, to make the back of the patchwork neat and eliminate unnecessary bulk. Just remember the rule: small pieces—large seam allowances, and you won't have any trouble.

Making Templates

Templates for straight-line patchwork are always accurate because you draw or photocopy the whole block. Any changes to the original block (whether by accident or intentional) will not result in inaccurate templates, because when the drawn or photocopied block is cut up, it will go back together perfectly.

The designs are shown on a grid of squares, indicated by dashed lines. By changing the size of the squares, you can enlarge the design to whatever size you need. For example, if the design is drawn on a grid of 8 x 8 squares and you make each square 1¼", the finished block will be 10" x 10". If you make each square 1½", the finished block will be 12" x 12".

The designs can be enlarged by drawing or photocopying.

To draw the block design:
1. For Baby Bear, draw a grid of squares 12 x 8, making each square ½". This will result in a 6" x 4" finished block size. For Mama and Papa bear, draw a grid of 12 x 8 squares, ¾" x ¾". This will result in a 9" x 6" finished block size. You can draw the grid on graph paper or on template plastic.

For drawing the grid squares, use a different-colored pencil or pen from the one you use to draw the design line, so you can distinguish between the grid lines and the design lines.

2. Use a pencil (or pen on template plastic) to draw the design onto the grid, using the grid to locate where the lines should be placed. Draw the longest lines first. It is easy to draw the lines if you first mark the ends of each line with a dot, then join the dots.

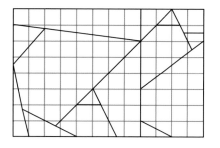

3. Mark each piece with its correct number.
4. Color or sketch a pattern onto the pieces, to help identify which pieces go with which fabrics. **09 bear**

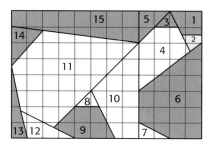

To photocopy the block design:

Yes, it is okay to photocopy the design for your own personal use. Usually, this is not recommended for making templates, because the process of photocopying distorts the templates slightly. The small distortions in one shape can add up to larger distortions when several shapes that have been photocopied are repeated or combined. But with the straight-line patchwork blocks, the whole block is being copied and therefore any distortions affect the whole block and do not change the accuracy of the final templates. You will find, however, that the outside edge of an enlarged pattern will not be totally accurate, so you will need to make some slight adjustments at the sides.

To enlarge the Bear block to a 9" x 6" block, enlarge the design by 150%:
1. Select the paper size to fit your enlarged design.
2. Set the photocopier to 150%.
3. Measure the photocopied design, and with a ruler and pencil, adjust the sides in or out as necessary to make the block exactly 9" x 6". Such alterations will not substantially change the design.

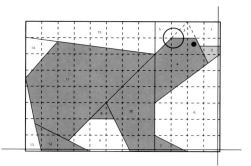

Now you are ready to transfer the design to your template material. Use either cardboard, such as tagboard, or template plastic.

NOTE: You've already completed this step if you have drawn the design directly onto the template plastic with a grid.

To use cardboard for templates:
1. Glue the photocopied or drawn design onto the cardboard, using a gluestick. Do not use other kinds of paste or glue, because they may wet and distort the paper.

NOTE: Do not cut out the pieces of the design and then glue them to cardboard; always glue the whole design onto cardboard.

2. Cut around the edges of the block, then cut out each piece. Cut longer lines first.
3. Mark grain lines on the wrong side of each template because templates are usually used right side down.

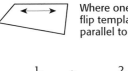

Where one edge is parallel to grain line, flip template over and mark with arrow parallel to edge.

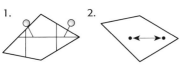

Where there is no edge parallel to grain line:
1. Push pins through template on grain line (grid line);
2. Flip template over to the reverse side and mark the grain line between the two pin holes.

To use template plastic for templates:
1. Tape or clip the design (either photocopy or drawing) under the plastic. Using a permanent marker and ruler, copy the design onto the plastic.
2. Copy the numbers onto each piece and sketch in a pattern to indicate which fabrics are to be used.
3. Copy grain lines onto the templates by copying at least one grid line onto each template piece, marking this line with an arrowhead at each end so you know it is the grain line. You will be able to see these lines through the plastic when you turn the template upside down to mark.
4. Cut around the edges of the block, then cut out each piece. Store your templates in large envelopes.

Marking and Cutting the Fabric

It is essential to mark all the seam lines for straight-line patchwork. But before marking the fabric, there are two essential points to consider:

1. *Which way the animal will face.* To make the design exactly as it is pictured on the page, place the templates, right side down, on the wrong side of the fabric so your pencil lines will be on the wrong side of the fabric. This is the reason templates must have the grain lines marked on their reverse sides. To make a reverse image of the block (animal facing the opposite way), place the templates right side up on the wrong side of the fabric. It is important to be clear about this before you begin to mark, so that all your marking for the block is consistent.

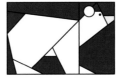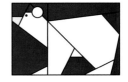

Mark with templates face down.

For reverse image, mark with templates face up.

2. *Grain line.* It is important to keep grain line in mind as you mark your fabrics. In patchwork, you want to keep the grain line consistent in a block wherever possible. In some instances, as when using a stripe, you may not be able to keep all the fabrics on-grain. These exceptions are usually not a problem if other pieces in the block are kept on-grain.

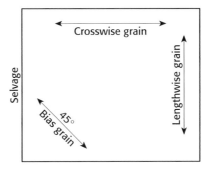

To mark and cut the pieces:

1. Sort all your templates into piles according to the fabrics you are using. Make a pile of the pieces that will be white (pieces 4, 7, 8, 10, 11, 12) and a pile for the background (pieces 1, 3, 5, 6, 9, 13, 14, 15). There will be one piece (piece 2) for the muzzle.

Background pieces   Muzzle   Bear pieces

2. Place the fabric on top of a sandpaper board (see page 6), right side down. Place a template, also right side down, on top of the fabric (or for the reverse image, place the template right side up). Match the grain of the fabric with the grain line marked on the template.

3. Leave a least ¾" between each piece so you have enough room to cut a ⅜"-wide seam allowance around each piece. For small pieces and long, pointed pieces, leave a generous 1" between pieces so you can cut a ½"-wide seam allowance. It is unnecessary to mark a cutting line. The seam allowance does not have to be measured since you will pin the pieces together along the marked seam line.

Cut out with ⅜"-wide seam allowances.

Cut out small and pointed pieces with ½"-wide seam allowances.

4. Using a sharp pencil, mark around the template, making sure that the corners are clearly marked.

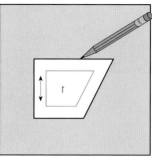

Mark with template,
right side down,
on wrong side of fabric.

5. Write the number of each piece in the seam allowance of the fabric, so you can identify the pieces after they have been cut out.

6. Cut out each piece and lay it out in its correct position. I find it easiest to lay out each piece after I cut it, rather than waiting to lay out all the pieces at once.

Pinning, Stitching, and Pressing

Just before you sew each seam, pin the pieces together, following this little three-step routine.

1. Push pins through at the corners. Pick up the two pieces to be pinned, keeping them

in their correct orientation to each other but placing them right sides together. Push a pin through the right-hand corner of the top piece, then turn the two pieces over and push the pin into the corner of the underneath piece. Repeat the procedure at the other corner.

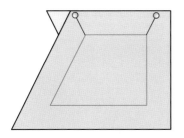

2. Pin at the corners. Holding the fabric pieces at both corners, where the pins are, gently adjust the pieces so the marked lines on both sides of the fabric match up. Anchor both pins by bringing the points up toward the center, not toward the other edges of the pieces.

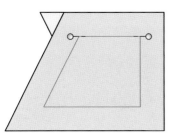

3. Place pins along the length of the marked line. Pin along the length of the seam, placing pins with their heads pointing to the right. Check both sides to be sure you are pinning along both lines exactly and make any adjustments as needed. Place an extra anchor pin parallel and below the pin at the left-hand corner. This pin will hold the pieces correctly when you take away the first pin as you begin stitching.

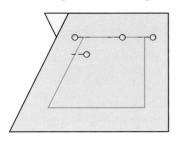

To machine piece and press:

1. Set the stitch length between 10 and 12 stitches per inch. This length gives a neat stitch, but one that is not too difficult to undo should a small correction be necessary.

2. Following the piecing order carefully, pick up the first two pieces to be stitched together and pin as described at left. Take out the pin in the left-hand corner and place the cut edge below the needle, lining up the needle with the marked line. Stitch from the cut edge, across the seam allowances, along the marked line, and across the seam allowances at the other side to the cut edges. As you sew, pull out the pins just before they go under the presser foot. Snip the thread ends and trim the seam allowances to an even ¼" after you have stitched the seam.

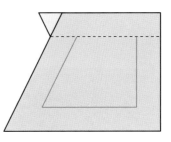

For machine piecing,
stitch from cut edge to cut edge
along marked line.

3. Press the seams to one side. Decide which side to press the seam allowances toward, based on the following considerations:
   • Press seams toward the dark fabric.
   • Press seams in the direction they naturally want to go. Especially where there are bulky seam intersections, some seam allowances have a mind of their own, so it is best to go with the flow.
   • Press seams away from the lines where quilting will be stitched.

4. When the block is complete, use your rotary cutter and large square ruler to trim the edges of the block, so it is exactly the size required, plus a ¼"-wide seam allowance all around.

To hand piece and press:
1. Following the piecing order carefully, pick up and pin pieces together before stitching as described on pages 54–55.
2. Thread your needle with a color to match the darker fabric. Tie a knot at the end of the thread.
3. Begin stitching ⅛" from one corner of the seam, take a small stitch into the exact corner, then turn and sew along the marked seam line with a running stitch. Pull the pins out as you come to them. When you reach the other corner, sew into it exactly, then turn and take a couple of stitches backward, ending with a back-stitch a short distance from the corner. Snip off the thread.

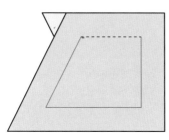

For hand piecing, stitch only
along marked line and
not into seam allowances.

4. Complete all seams in this manner, following the piecing order. Note that you should not be sewing into any seam allowances (as you would if you were machine piecing); all seam allowances should be left free. When you come to a cross seam, sew right up to it, then push your needle through the seam allowances, leaving them upright, and begin sewing on the other side.

5. Trim the seam allowances and press them together toward one side, as described for machine piecing.
6. Trim the edges of the block so it is exactly the size you need, plus ¼" seam allowance all around.

Bear Block (8 x 12 squares)

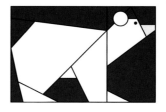

Finished Size: 6" x 4"
> Draw or photocopy block as shown on facing page; each square = ½"

Finished Size: 9" x 6"
> To enlarge from the grid, each square = ¾"
> To enlarge by photocopying, enlarge by 150%.

Color Key

Muzzle (off-white) – 2
Body (white) – 4, 7, 8, 10, 11, 12
Background – 1, 3, 5, 6, 9, 13, 14, 15

Piecing Section One

A. 1 + 2
B. 3 + 4
C. (1–2) + (3–4) + 5
D. (1–5) + 6 + 7

Piecing Section Two

E. 8 + 9
F. (8–9) + 10
G. (8–10) + 11
H. (8–11) + 12
I. (8–12) + 13 + 14
J. (8–14) + 15

Piecing Section Three

K. (1–7) + (8–15)
L. Appliqué ear.

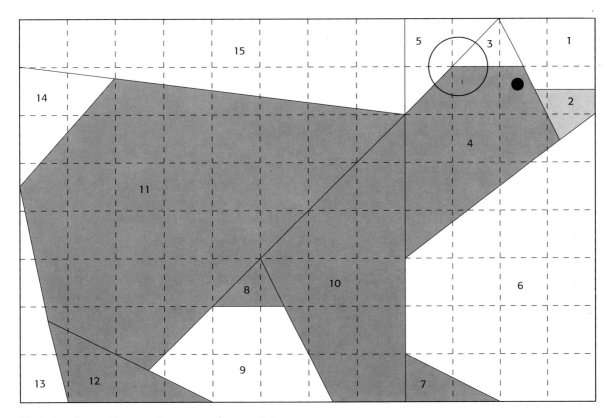

Block size shown: 6" x 4"   1 square as shown = ½"

Bear Block Assembly

1. Cut and piece the Bear blocks, using the straight-line patchwork technique described on pages 50–56.
2. Appliqué white circle (on pattern) for bear's ear.
3. Trim the Baby Bear block to 6½" x 4½". Trim Mama and Papa Bear blocks to 9½" x 6½".

Tree Block (4 x 7 squares)

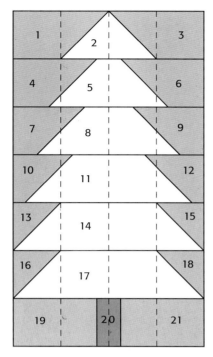

1 square as shown = ½"

Finished Size: 6" x 10½"

To enlarge from the grid, each square = 1½"

To enlarge by photocopying, enlarge by 300% in 3 steps:

1. 150%
2. 150%
3. 133%

Color Key

Tree (green) – 2, 5, 8, 11, 14, 17
Background – 1, 3, 4, 6, 7, 9, 10, 12, 13, 15, 16, 18, 19, 21
Trunk (brown) – 20

Piecing Order

A. 1 + 2 + 3
B. 4 + 5 + 6
C. 7 + 8 + 9
D. 10 + 11 + 12
E. 13 + 14 + 15
F. 16 + 17 + 18
G. 19 + 20 + 21
H. (1–3) + (4–6) + (7–9) + (10–12) + (13–15) + (16–18) + (19–21)

Tree Block Assembly

1. Cut and piece the Tree blocks, using the straight-line patchwork technique described on pages 50–56. For the smaller tree, eliminate pieces 16, 17, and 18.
2. Trim the large Tree block to 6½" x 11", and the small Tree block to 6½" x 9½".

Quilt Assembly and Finishing

1. From the navy blue print, cut:
   1 rectangle, 6½" x 9", for above Baby Bear
   2 rectangles, 7" x 9½", for above Mama and Papa Bear
   1 rectangle, 4" x 6½", for above short tree
   1 rectangle, 2½" x 6½", for above tall tree
   1 strip, 2½" x 13", for between trees

2. Join Bear blocks, Tree blocks, and background pieces as shown below. All measurements in the illustration include ¼"-wide seam allowances.

3. **From the green print, cut:**
   2 strips, 1½" x 13", for inner side borders
   2 strips, 1½" x 40½", for inner top and bottom border
   From the blue/white print, cut:
   2 strips, 3¾" x 15, for outer side borders
   2 strips, 3¾" x 47", for outer top and bottom border

4. Referring to "Straight-Cut Borders" on pages 11–12, measure, trim, and sew the inner border strips to the side edges first, then to the top and bottom edges. Repeat with the outer border strips.

5. Layer the quilt top with batting and backing; baste. Quilt as desired.

6. Add star buttons to the trees and sky. Sew on buttons for eyes.

7. Tie a knot in one end of the 6" piece of ribbon to make a scarf for Papa Bear. Tack in place above and below neck.

8. Add pompons to Baby Bear and Mama Bear for earmuffs.

9. Cut 4 strips, 2" x 42", from the navy blue/white print for binding. Bind the edges and add a label.

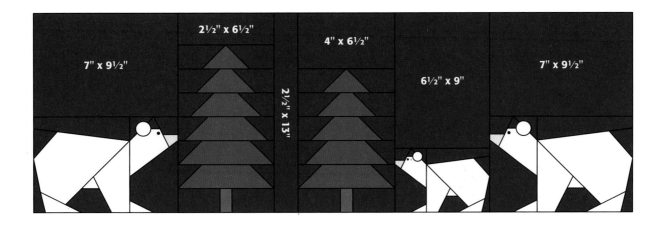

Poinsettia Star *by Christina Wright, 1999, Woodinville, Washington, 36½" x 48½".*

Poinsettia Star

Vibrant poinsettia blooms adorn an Eight-Pointed Star block in this wall hanging by Senior Customer Service Representative Christina Wright. The corner poinsettias were fussy-cut, fused, and quilted with gold thread, adding delicate texture to the overall design. The pattern, "Hollyberry Star," comes from *Calendar Quilts* by Joan Hanson.

Finished Quilt Size: 36½" x 48½"

MATERIALS: 44"-wide fabric

1 yd. poinsettia print for block, appliqué, and binding
½ yd. light print for background
¾ yd. green print for block, second border, and checkerboard
⅛ yd. red/green stripe for first border
⅓ yd. red/gold print for checkerboard
⅓ yd. gold print for third border
⅔ yd. red print for fourth border
1½ yds. for backing
⅓ yd. paper-backed fusible web

Cutting

Cut strips across the width of the fabric.

From the poinsettia print, cut:
4 squares, 4⅞" x 4⅞"; cut squares once diagonally to yield 8 half-square triangles for piece C
1 square, 6⅛" x 6⅛", for piece D
6 strips, 2" x 42", for binding

From the light print, cut:
4 squares 4½" x 4½", for piece A
1 square, 9¼" x 9¼", cut square twice diagonally to yield 4 quarter-square triangles for piece B
2 squares, 9⅞" x 9⅞"; cut squares once diagonally to yield 4 half-square triangles for corner triangles

From the green print, cut:
2 squares, 4⅞" x 4⅞"; cut squares once diagonally to yield 4 half-square triangles for piece E
3 strips, 2½" x 42", for checkerboard
8 strips, 2½" x 15", for second border

From the red/green stripe, cut:
2 strips, 2" x 42"; cut strips in half to make 4 strips, 2" x 21", for first border

From the red/gold print, cut:
3 strips, 2½" x 42", for checkerboard

From the gold print, cut:
4 strips, 2" x 42", for third border

From the red print, cut:
5 strips, 4" x 42", for fourth border

From the fabric for binding, cut:
5 strips, 2" x 42"

Block Assembly

1. Join 2 poinsettia print triangles (C) and a light print triangle (B).

Make 4.

2. Join 4 green print triangles (E) and the poinsettia print square (D).

Make 1.

3. Piece the center block.

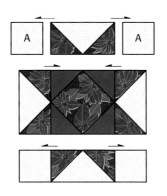

Quilt Assembly and Finishing

1. Sew the 4 strips of red/green stripe to the sides of the block for the first border. Refer to pages 12–13 for mitering corners. The strips are slightly oversized; trim the stripe border equally on all sides so that the block measures 18⅞" square. A handy way to do this is to use your 6" x 24" and 15" x 15" acrylic rulers side by side.

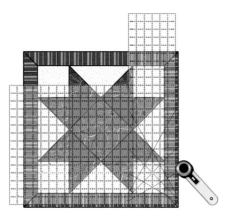

2. Sew the green print strips to the short sides of the large light print triangles, mitering the corners. Trim the ends of the border even with the long side of the triangle.

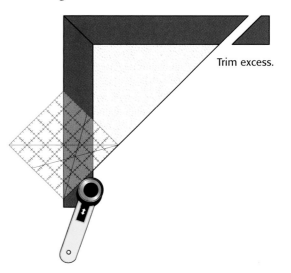

Trim excess.

3. Sew the 4 bordered triangles to the center square. The square should now measure 26½" x 26½".

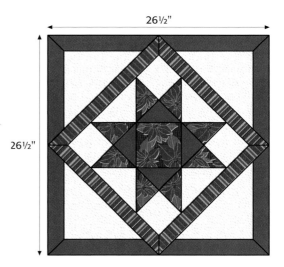

26½"

26½"

4. Iron paper-backed fusible web to the wrong side of a poinsettia-print piece large enough to include 12 flowers. Cut out 12 flowers and arrange 3 each on the corner triangles. Iron the flowers in place. If desired, sew with a small zigzag stitch around the raw edges.

5. To create the checkerboard sections, sew red/gold and green strips together to make 1 each of Strip Unit 1 and Strip Unit 2. From Strip Unit 1, cut 14 segments, 2½" wide. From Strip Unit 2, cut 12 segments, 2½" wide.

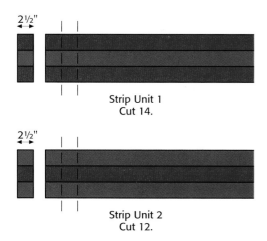

2½"

Strip Unit 1
Cut 14.

2½"

Strip Unit 2
Cut 12.

6. Arrange and sew together 13 segments to make each checkerboard section.

Make 2.

7. Sew the checkerboard sections to the opposite sides of the center section.

8. Referring to "Borders with Mitered Corners" on pages 12–13, measure the quilt top for mitered borders. Join the red print strips for the fourth border to make one continuous strip. Sew the gold print strips for the third border to the red strips for the fourth border and treat them as one. Sew the combined border strips to the quilt, mitering the corners.

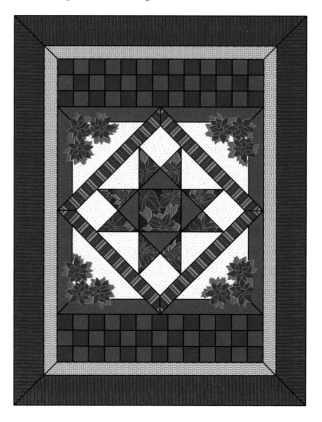

9. Layer the quilt with batting and backing; baste. Quilt as desired.

10. Bind the edges and add a label.

Gifts from the Heart *by Terry Martin, 1999, Snohomish, Washington, 52 ⅞" x 69 ⅞". Machine quilted by Sue Lohse.*

Gifts from the Heart

A holiday theme print creates a festive focal point for these tiled blocks, stitched in the more subdued holiday hues of dark berry and forest green. This cozy-up-by-the-fire quilt was created by Terry Martin, our Editorial Administrative Assistant. The pattern is "Stacked Tiles" from *Nifty Ninepatches* by Carolann Palmer.

Finished Quilt Size: 52⅞" x 69⅞"
Finished Block Size: 6"

MATERIALS: 44"-wide fabric

2 yds. large-scale Christmas print for blocks, outer border, and binding
1⅛ yds. light print for blocks
1 yd. burgundy print for blocks
1 yd. dark green print for blocks
½ yd light green print for blocks
⅜ yd. burgundy/green print for inner border
4¼ yds. for backing

Cutting

Cut strips across the width of the fabric.

From the Christmas print, cut:
5 strips, 4¾" x 42"; crosscut strips into 35 squares, 4¾" x 4¾", for Blocks B and C
6 strips, 4½" x 42", for outer border
7 strips, 2" x 42", for binding

From the light print, cut:
8 strips, 2 ½" x 42", for strip sets
2 strips, 4" x 42"; crosscut strips into 12 squares, 4" x 4". Cut squares twice diagonally to yield 48 quarter-square triangles for Blocks D, E, and F.

From the burgundy print, cut:
5 strips, 2½" x 42", for strip sets
4 strips, 3⅞" x 42"; crosscut strips into 36 squares, 3⅞" x 3⅞". Cut squares once diagonally to yield 72 half-square triangles for Block B.
4 squares, 2½" x 2½", for Block F

From the dark green print, cut:
6 strips, 2½" x 42"; crosscut 2 strips into 20 squares, 2½" x 2½", for Blocks D and E; reserve the remainder for strip sets
4 strips, 3⅞" x 42"; crosscut strips into 34 squares, 3⅞" x 3⅞". Cut squares once diagonally to yield 68 half-square triangles for Block C.

From the light green print, cut:
2 strips, 2½" x 42", for strip sets
1 strip, 4" x 42"; crosscut strip into 5 squares, 4" x 4". Cut squares twice diagonally to yield 20 quarter-square triangles for Blocks D and E
2 squares, 2½" x 2½"; cut squares once diagonally to yield 4 half-square triangles for Block F

From the burgundy/green print, cut:
5 strips, 1½" x 42", for inner border

Block Assembly

1. Join 2½"-wide strips as shown to make 3 of Strip Set 1 and 2 of Strip Set 2. From Strip Set 1, cut 48 segments, 2½" wide. From Strip Set 2, cut 24 segments, 2½" wide.

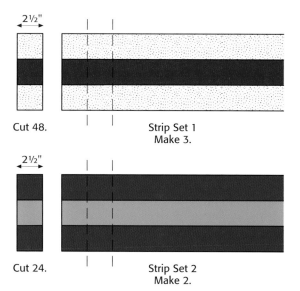

Cut 48. Strip Set 1 Make 3.

Cut 24. Strip Set 2 Make 2.

2. Join the segments from step 1 to make a Nine Patch block (Block A).

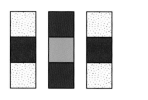

Block A
Make 24.

3. Join 4 burgundy triangles and a Christmas-print square to make Block B.

Block B
Make 18.

4. Join 4 dark green triangles and a Christmas-print square to make Block C.

Block C
Make 17.

5. Join the remaining 2½"-wide light and burgundy strips to make 2 strip sets. From the strip sets, cut 20 segments, 2½" wide.

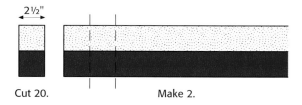

Cut 20. Make 2.

6. Join a segment from step 5, a dark green square, a light green triangle, and 2 light triangles to make Block D.

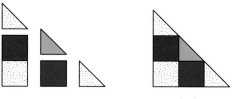

Block D
Make 10.

7. Join a segment from step 5, a dark green square, a light green triangle, and 2 light triangles to make Block E.

Block E
Make 10.

8. Join a burgundy square, 2 light triangles, and a light green triangle to make Block F.

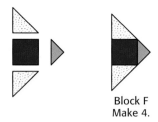

Block F
Make 4.

Quilt Assembly and Finishing

1. Arrange the blocks in diagonal rows. Sew the blocks into rows, pressing the seams in each row toward Block A and the side triangles. Join the rows, adding Block F to the corners last.

2. Referring to "Straight-Cut Borders" on pages 11–12, measure, trim, and sew the inner border strips to the side edges of the quilt top first, then to the top and bottom edges. Repeat for the outer borders.

3. Layer the quilt top with batting and backing; baste. Quilt as desired.

4. Bind the edges and add a label.

Family Reunion

Throughout this traditional-style holiday runner, Editorial Director Mary Green quilted beautiful poinsettias in a bold red perle cotton for an especially striking effect. She used the time-honored Union block from *101 Fabulous Rotary-Cut Quilts* by Nancy J. Martin and Judy Hopkins; the on-point setting is Mary's original design.

Finished Quilt Size: 18⅞" x 55⅝"
Finished Block Size: 12"

Family Reunion *by Mary Green, 1999, Monroe, Washington, 18⅞" x 55⅝".*

MATERIALS: 44"-wide fabric

1 yd. white print for blocks and side and
corner triangles

⅝ yd. red poinsettia print for blocks

½ yd. dark green print for blocks and
binding

1¾ yds. for backing

Cutting

Cut strips across the width of the fabric.

From the white print, cut:

2 strips, 3" x 42"; crosscut strips into 24
squares, 3" x 3", for half-square triangle
units

1 strip, 3¾" x 24"; crosscut strip into 6
squares, 3¾" x 3¾"; cut squares once
diagonally to yield 12 half-square triangles for piece B

1 strip, 2½" x 42"; crosscut strip into 12
squares, 2½" x 2½", for piece C

1 square, 19⅝" x 19⅝"; cut square twice
diagonally to yield 4 quarter-square
triangles for side triangles

2 squares, 10⅛" x 10⅛"; cut squares once
diagonally to yield 4 half-square triangles for corner triangles

From the red poinsettia print, cut:
   2 strips, 3" x 42"; crosscut strips into 24 squares, 3" x 3", for half-square triangle units
   6 strips, 1" x 12½", for block border
   6 strips, 1" x 13½", for block border
   3 squares, 4½" x 4½", for piece A

From the dark green print, cut:
   1 strip, 4⅞" x 42"; crosscut strip into 6 squares, 4⅞" x 4⅞"; cut squares once diagonally to yield 12 half-square triangles for piece D
   4 strips, 2" x 42", for binding

Block Assembly

1. Draw a diagonal line on the wrong side of each 3" square. Place a white square on top of a red print square, right sides together. Sew ¼" from the drawn line on both sides. Cut on the drawn line. Press the seam toward the red print triangle.

Make 48.

2. Trim the square to 2½" x 2½". Place a square ruler's diagonal line on the diagonal seam line and trim from all 4 sides.

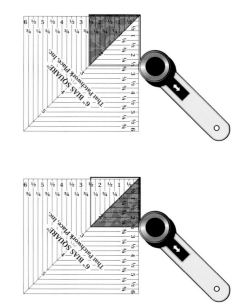

NOTE: Sewing together triangles that are larger than needed and then trimming to the required size after stitching results in more accurately sized units.

3. Piece a Union Square block as shown.

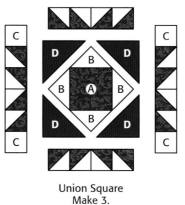

Union Square
Make 3.

4. Sew a 1" x 12½" red print strip to opposite sides of each block. Sew a 1" x 13½" red print strip to the remaining sides of each block.

Quilt Assembly and Finishing

1. Arrange the blocks and the side and corner triangles in diagonal rows. Sew the blocks and side triangles together in rows. Join the rows, adding the corner triangles last.
2. Layer the quilt top with batting and backing; baste. Quilt as desired. Mary quilted her runner with red perle cotton to make the quilting design more prominent. The poinsettia centers are French knots made with gold metallic perle cotton.
3. Bind the edges and add a label.

Seeing Is Believing *by Carol Atterberry, 1999, Monroe, Washington, 41½" x 41½".*

Seeing Is Believing

An animated conversation print featuring Santa and friends fills the windows of this whimsical holiday quilt by Carol Atterberry, Customer Service Representative. The pattern, "Easy Attic Windows," is from *Quilts for Baby: Easy as ABC* by Ursula Reikes.

Finished Quilt Size: 41½" x 41½"
Finished Block Size: 8"

MATERIALS: 44"-wide fabric

½ yd. feature fabric
½ yd. red solid for blocks* and border
⅜ yd. green solid for blocks*
½ yd. black/gold print for sashing and inner border
⅜ yd. red/white check for middle border
¾ yd. Christmas print for outer border
1¼ yds. for backing
⅜ yd. for binding*

*If you prefer to make a two-color binding as shown in the photo, buy an extra ¼ yard each of the red and green solids instead of the ⅜ yard for binding.

Cutting

Cut strips across the width of the fabric.

From the feature fabric, cut:
  9 squares, 6½" x 6½"

From the red solid, cut:
  2 strips, 2½" x 42"; crosscut strips into 9 rectangles, 2½" x 6½", for piece A
  1 strip, 3" x 42"; crosscut strip into 5 squares, 3" x 3". Cut squares once diagonally to yield 10 half-square triangles. You will use only 9.
  2 strips, ¾" x 31½", for third side border
  2 strips, ¾" x 32", for third top and bottom border

From the green solid, cut:
  2 strips, 2½" x 42"; crosscut strips into 9 rectangles, 2½" x 6½", for piece B
  1 strip, 3" x 42"; crosscut strip into 5 squares, 3" x 3". Cut squares once diagonally to yield 10 half-square triangles. You will use only 9.

From the black/gold print, cut:
  3 strips, 1½" x 42"; crosscut strips into 2 pieces, 1½" x 26½", for horizontal sashing between rows, and 6 pieces, 1½" x 8½", for vertical sashing strips between blocks
  2 strips, 1½" x 26½", for first side border
  2 strips, 1½" x 28½", for first top and bottom border

From the red/white check, cut:
  2 strips, 2" x 28½", for second side border
  2 strips, 2" x 31½", for second top and bottom border**

From the Christmas print, cut:
  2 strips, 5½" x 32", for fourth side border
  2 strips, 5½" x 42", for fourth top and bottom border

**Carol used a border print with the word "Believe" in it for the middle top and bottom borders. If you can find such a print, you can substitute it for the red/white check on the top and bottom.

From the fabric for binding, cut:
    5 strips, 2" x 42"***

***If making a two-color binding, cut 2½ strips, 2" wide, from each of the red and green solids instead of the 5 strips.

Block Assembly

1. Join a red triangle and a green triangle to make a half-square triangle unit. Trim the squares to 2½" x 2½". Place a ruler's diagonal line on the diagonal seam line and trim from all 4 sides.

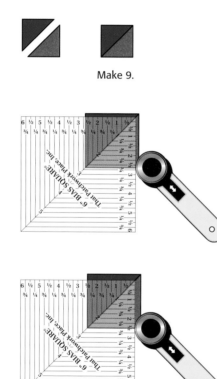

Make 9.

2. Piece the Attic Window block as shown.

Make 9.

Quilt Assembly and Finishing

1. Sew 3 blocks and 2 vertical sashing strips together to make each row. Make 3 rows. Press the seams toward the sashing.

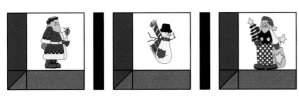

Make 3.

2. Join the rows, adding the horizontal sashing strips between them. Press the seams toward the sashing.

3. Referring to "Straight-Cut Borders" on pages 11–12, measure, trim, and sew the first border strips to the side edges of the quilt top first, then to the top and bottom edges. Repeat for the second, third, and fourth borders.
4. Layer the quilt top with batting and backing; baste. Quilt as desired.
5. Bind the edges and add a label. To make the two-color binding as shown in the photo, join 2"-wide strips for binding, end to end, alternating red and green strips. Add a half strip to a 42" strip of the same color. Sew the binding to the quilt, starting in the middle of one of the sides.

Mr. Snowman *by Laurel Strand, 1999, Everett, Washington, 13½" x 17½".*

Mr. Snowman

Lead Illustrator Laurel Strand appliquéd this snowman by hand using a buttonhole stitch, then added a touch of Christmas plaid in the border. The original "Mr. Snowman" can be found in *Celebrate with Little Quilts* by Alice Berg, Sylvia Johnson, and Mary Ellen Von Holt.

Finished Quilt Size: 13½" x 17½"

MATERIALS: 44"-wide fabric

6" x 9" piece of white-on-white print for snowman
9½" x 10½" piece of green print for background
Scrap of red print for scarf
Scrap of dark green print for hat
⅛ yd. green-and-red plaid for triangles
⅛ yd. light print for triangles
¼ yd. red print for border and binding
½ yd. for backing
15" x 20" piece of thin batting
Black, red, and white embroidery floss
Buttons: 3 assorted medium, 2 tiny black, and 1 carrot for nose
12" of ⅛"-wide black ribbon for hatband

Cutting

Cut strips across the width of the fabric.

From the green-and-red plaid, cut:
6 squares, 2½" x 2½". Cut the squares once diagonally to yield 12 half-square triangles.

From the light print, cut:
6 squares, 2½" x 2½". Cut the squares once diagonally to yield 12 half-square triangles.

From the red print, cut:
4 strips, 2½" x 13½", for border
2 strips, 2" x 42", for binding

Block Assembly

Use snowman, scarf, and hat templates on page 79.
1. From the white-on-white print, cut 1 snowman.
2. Pin the snowman to the 9½" x 10½" green print background. Refer to the illustration below for placement. Buttonhole-stitch around the edges.

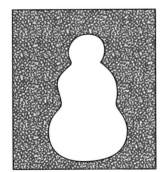

Buttonhole Stitch

If the background fabric shows through the snowman, either cut a second snowman from white fabric and place it behind the white-on-white fabric before stitching, or carefully cut away the background fabric behind him after stitching, leaving a ¼"-wide seam allowance all around.
3. Pin the scarf in place and buttonhole-stitch around the edges.
4. Cut the ⅛"-wide ribbon into 3 pieces, 4" long, and braid them together to make a piece approximately 2" long. Appliqué the braid to the hat.

5. Pin the hat in place and buttonhole-stitch around the edges.

Quilt Assembly and Finishing

1. Join a plaid triangle and a light triangle to make a half-square triangle unit. Trim the squares to 2" x 2". Place a ruler's diagonal line on the diagonal seam line and trim from all 4 sides.

Make 12.

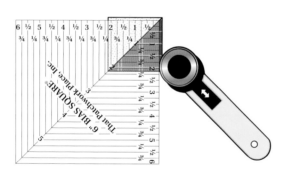

2. Join 6 half-square triangle units to form a row.

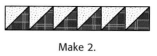

Make 2.

3. Sew a row of triangles to the top and bottom edges of the Snowman block. Press the seams toward the Snowman block.
4. Sew the red 2½" x 13½" strips to the side edges of the Snowman block first, then to the top and bottom edges.

5. Layer the quilt top with batting and backing; baste. Quilt as desired.
6. Bind the edges and add a label.
7. Sew buttons on the snowman, referring to the quilt photo on page 76 for placement. Stitch a row of French knots for the mouth.

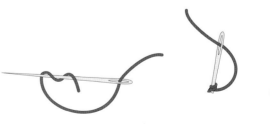

French Knot

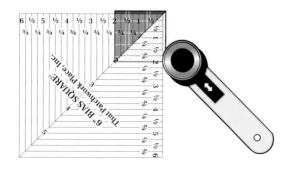

Hat

Hatband placement

Scarf

Snowman

**Mr. Snowman
Templates**

Add ¼"-wide seam allowances
to appliqué templates.

Christmas Infinity *by Linda Thomas, 1999, Everett, Washington, 40½" x 40½".*

Christmas Infinity

Sales Representative Linda Thomas challenged her Christmas color sense with this pattern, "Cotton Candy Weave," from *Designing Quilts: The Value of Value* by Suzanne Hammond. The jewel-toned interlocking pattern creates a fascinating three-dimensional effect.

Finished Quilt Size: 40½" x 40½"
Finished Block Size: 4"

MATERIALS: 44"-wide fabric

- 6" x 12" piece each of 12 different dark greens
- 6" x 12" piece each of 12 different dark reds
- 6" x 12" piece each of 12 different dark golds
- 3" x 3" square of 6 different medium greens
- 3" x 3" square of 6 different medium reds
- 3" x 3" square of 6 different medium golds
- 1⅛ yds. light print for blocks, border, and binding
- 1⅓ yds. for backing

Cutting

Cut strips across the width of the fabric.

From *each* of the dark fabrics, cut:
- 1 square, 4⅞" x 4⅞" (36 total); cut squares once diagonally to yield 2 half-square triangles (72 total)
- 2 squares, 2½" x 2½" (72 total)

From *each* of the medium fabrics, cut:
- 1 square, 2⅞" x 2⅞" (18 total); cut squares once diagonally to yield 2 half-square triangles (36 total)

From the light print, cut:
- 4 strips, 2½" x 42", for border
- 9 squares, 4½" x 4½"
- 4 strips, 2⅞" x 42"; crosscut strips into 54 squares, 2⅞" x 2⅞". Cut squares once diagonally to yield 108 half-square triangles
- 5 strips, 2" x 42", for binding

Block Assembly

Before assembling the blocks, arrange the pieces on your design wall, starting with the large triangles and plain center squares. Use large triangles in the same color family within the green and red loop and the gold square.

Add the small squares next. Place the small medium-value triangles in their proper color positions according to the diagram below. These medium fabrics strengthen the weave design and also create the pinwheel centers. Fill in the rest of the quilt top with the small background triangles.

1. Join 2 small light triangles and a dark square. Press the seam allowances toward the square. Be careful to avoid stretching the bias edges.

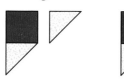

2. Join a pieced triangle and a large dark triangle to complete a block. Press the seam allowance toward the large triangle.

Be careful to keep each block in the proper sequence. Square up the sides of the blocks as you complete them and return them to their correct position.

Quilt Assembly and Finishing

1. Sew the blocks together into horizontal rows. Join the rows.

2. Referring to "Straight-Cut Borders" on pages 11–12, measure, trim, and sew the border strips to the side edges of the quilt top first, then to the top and bottom edges.
3. Layer the quilt top with batting and backing; baste. Quilt as desired.
4. Bind the edges and add a label.

Starstruck

Five elaborate star blocks set on point in warm, inviting country colors make for a gorgeous Christmas wall quilt by Office Manager Kathy Culley. The striking star patterns are taken from *All-Star Sampler* by Roxanne Carter.

Finished Quilt Size: 58½" x 58½"
Finished Block Size: 12"

Starstruck *by Kathy Culley, 1999, Woodinville, Washington, 58½" x 58½". Quilted by Roxanne Carter.*

MATERIALS: 44"-wide fabric

Fabric 1 1½ yds. Christmas print for blocks, outer border, and binding

Fabric 2 ⅜ yd. green print for blocks

Fabric 3 ⅜ yd. beige print for blocks

Fabric 4 ¾ yd. red print #1 for blocks and inner border

Fabric 5 1 yd. red print #2 for blocks and sashing

Fabric 6 ⅜ yd. green/beige check for blocks

Fabric 7 ⅜ yd. beige/green stripe for blocks

Fabric 8 ½ yd. white solid for background in blocks

⅛ yd. red/green plaid for cornerstones

⅞ yd. white/gold print for side and corner triangles

3⅜ yds. for backing

Cutting Sashing and Borders

Cut strips across the width of the fabric. Refer to the individual blocks on pages 86–93 for cutting block pieces.

From the Christmas print, cut:
6 strips, 4" x 42", for outer border
6 strips, 2" x 42", for binding

From red print #1, cut:
5 strips, 2" x 42", for inner border

From red print #2, cut:
6 strips, 3" x 42"; crosscut strips into a total of 16 segments, 3" x 12½", for sashing

From the red/green plaid, cut:
1 strip, 3" x 42"; crosscut strip into 12 squares, 3" x 3", for cornerstones

From the white/gold print, cut:
1 square, 21⅞" x 21⅞"; cut square twice diagonally to yield 4 quarter-square triangles for side triangles
2 squares, 13" x 13"; cut squares once diagonally to yield 4 half-square triangles for corner triangles

Cutting Diamonds

1. Cut strips from selected fabrics in the width indicated for the block.
2. Cut the diamonds the same width as the width of the strips. Place the ruler's 45° line on the edge of the strip. Trim the selvage end of the strips at a 45° angle.

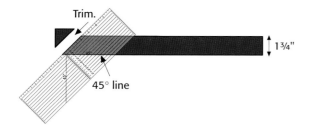

3. To cut the diamonds, place the ruler's 45°-angle line at the edge of the strip and the required measurement on your ruler at the cut edge of the strip. If the strip width is 1¾", cut the diamonds 1¾" wide.

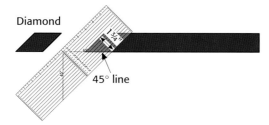

Sewing Set-In Seams

Use a ruler and pencil to mark the ¼" intersections of all pieces. Use a pin to match the ¼" marks at each corner when joining pieces. Follow the piecing diagram to stitch the pieces together. The ¼" marks are indicated in the illustrations with a dot. Always backstitch when you start or stop a seam at a ¼" mark.

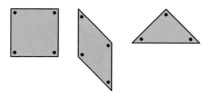

A small dot on the piece indicates the point to start stitching, and the arrow indicates the direction to stitch. If there is no dot at the other end of the piece, continue stitching all the way to the edge.

A small dot at both ends of a piece indicates that you need to stitch from dot to dot. Do not stitch beyond the dots.

The number next to the arrows between pieces indicates the order in which to sew the seams. Always start with seam 1.

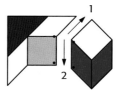

Dutch Rose

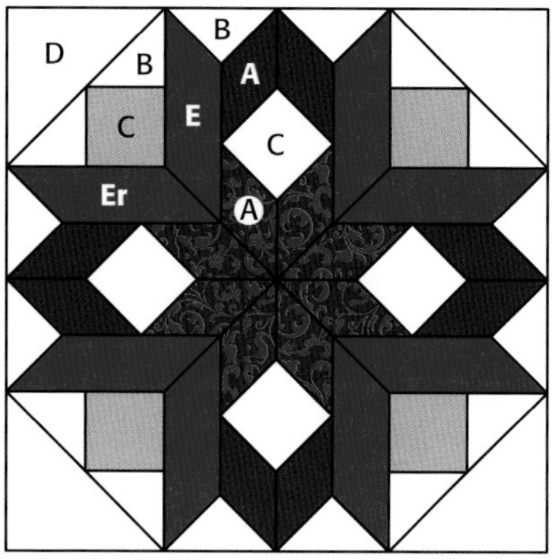

D
B
B
A
C
E
C
Er
A

Cutting

Fabric	Piece	Cut
1	A	8 diamonds from 1¾"-wide strips
2	A	8 diamonds from 1¾"-wide strips
3	C	4 squares, 2¼" x 2¼"
4	E	1 strip, 1¾" x 42"; fold strip in half, wrong sides together. Cut 4 segments, 3" wide, at a 45° angle. You will get 4 piece E and 4 piece E reversed.

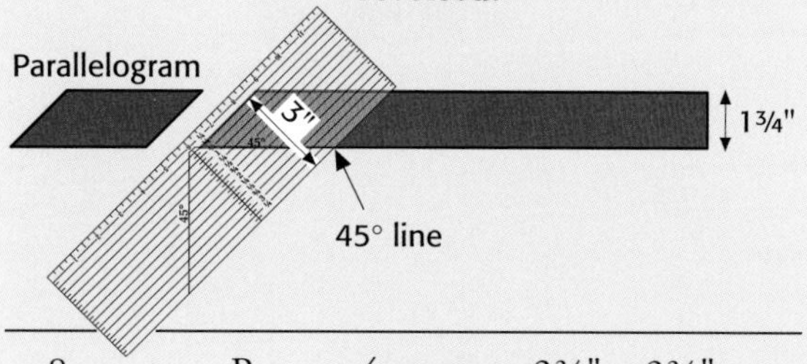

Parallelogram
3"
1¾"
45° line

Fabric	Piece	Cut
8	B	4 squares, 3¾" x 3¾"; cut twice diagonally to yield 16 quarter-square triangles
8	C	4 squares, 2¼" x 2¼"
8	D	2 squares, 4⅜" x 4⅜"; cut once diagonally to yield 4 half-square triangles

Block Assembly

1. Sew 2 Fabric #1 diamonds (A) to the sides of a 2¼" background square (C). Match the points of the diamonds and stitch. Trim the tips of the diamonds that extend beyond the seam allowance. Press the seams of the diamonds to one side, and the seams of the square toward the diamonds. Press the seams of the diamonds in the same direction around the block.

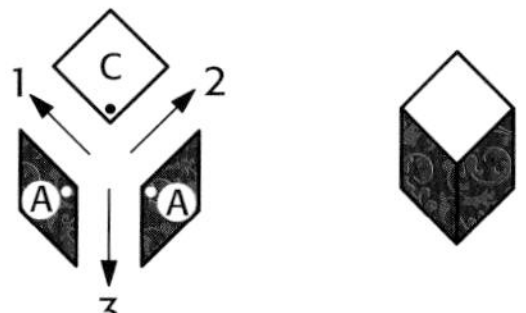

C
1
2
A
A
3

Make 4.

2. Sew 2 Fabric #2 diamonds to the remaining sides of the background square (C) in the same manner to complete the center unit.

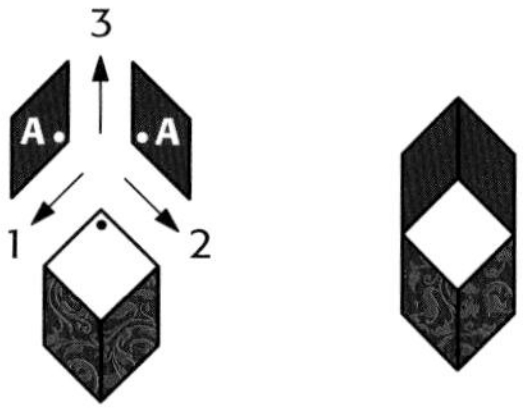

3
A
A
1
2

Center Unit
Make 4.

3. Sew the short sides of 2 small background triangles (B) to the sides of a 2¼" Fabric #3 square (C). Sew this unit to a large background triangle (D). Press the seam allowances toward the large triangle.

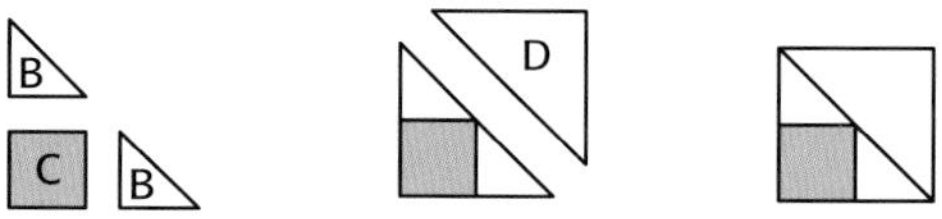

B
C
B
D

Make 4.

4. Sew a Fabric #4 parallelogram (E) to one side of the corner unit. Repeat with a reverse parallelogram (Er) on the adjacent side of the corner unit as shown. Match the points of the parallelogram and stitch. Trim the tips of the parallelogram extending beyond the seam allowances; press the seam allowances to one side.

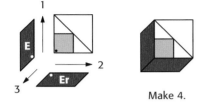

Make 4.

5. Sew the short side of a small background triangle (B) to the end of each parallelogram (E) to complete the corner unit.

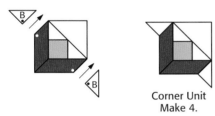

Corner Unit
Make 4.

6. Sew 2 center units to the sides of a corner unit.

 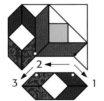

Make 2.

7. Join the units to complete the block. Stitch the seams in numerical order. If the seam allowances of the diamonds were pressed in the same direction, they will butt together easily, creating a nice, clean join.

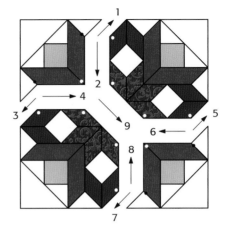

Blazing Star

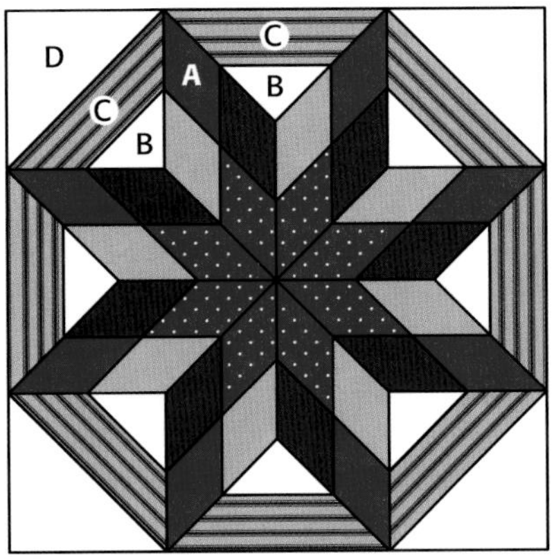

D
A
C
B
C
B

Cutting

Cut diamonds from strips, following the directions on page 85.

Fabric	Piece	Cut
2	A	1 strip, 1¾" x 42"
3	A	1 strip, 1¾" x 42"
4	A	1 strip, 1¾" x 42"
5	A	1 strip, 1¾" x 42"
7	C	2 squares, 6¼" x 6¼"; cut twice diagonally to yield 8 quarter-square triangles
8	B	4 squares, 2⅝" x 2⅝"; cut once diagonally to yield 8 half-square triangles
8	D	2 squares, 4⅜" x 4⅜"; cut once diagonally to yield 4 half-square triangles

Block Assembly

1. Sew the 1¾"-wide A strips together, staggering the seams about 1", to make 2 strip sets. Align the 45° line on the ruler with a horizontal seam and cut one end at a 45° angle. Cut 8 segments, 1¾" wide, from each strip set, making each cut parallel to the first cut.

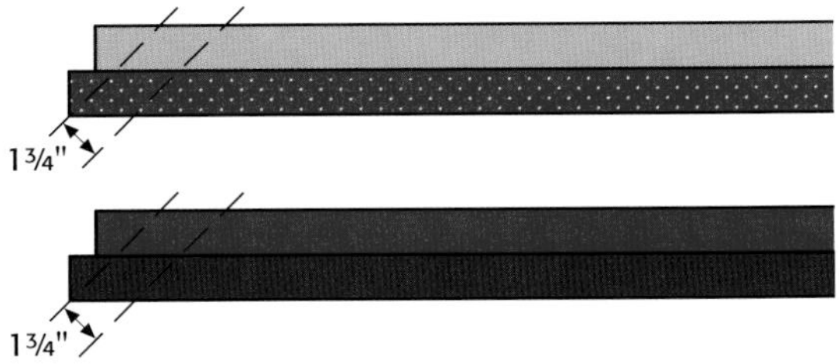

1¾"
1¾"

2. Matching the seams, sew a segment from each strip unit together to make a diamond unit.

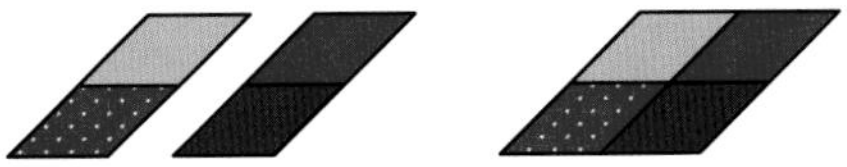

Diamond Unit
Make 8.

3. To make a trapezoid (C), place the ruler's 1¾" mark on the long edge of a Fabric #7 quarter-square triangle. Use a rotary cutter to trim the corner.

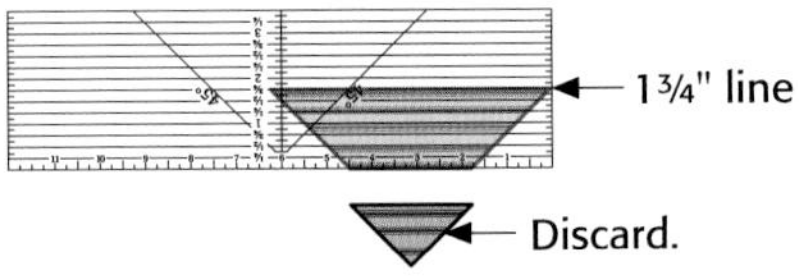

1¾" line
Discard.

Cut 8.

4. Sew a small background triangle (B) to the short side of a Fabric #7 trapezoid (C). To each of 4 B/C units, sew a large background triangle (D) to make a corner unit. Press the seams toward the trapezoid. Use the remaining 4 B/C units for the side triangles.

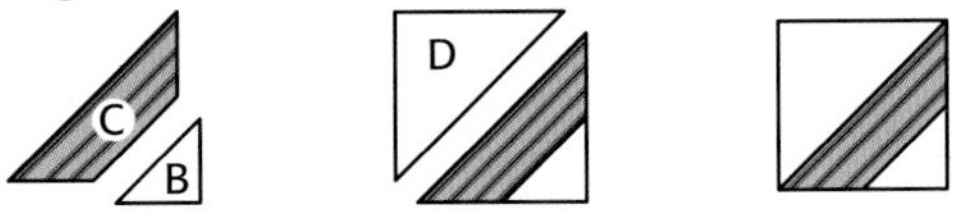

C
B
D

Side Triangle
Make 8.

Corner Square
Make 4.

5. Arrange the diamonds, side triangles (B/C), and corner units (B/C/D). Sew the units together, following the directions below for constructing an eight-pointed star.

Constructing an Eight-Pointed Star

Don't forget to mark the ¼" intersections on all diamonds, squares, and triangles. Start and stop stitching at the ¼" marks on the pieces as indicated in the piecing diagrams.

1. Sew a triangle to a diamond. Use a pin to match the ¼" marks on each of the 2 pieces. Begin stitching at the ¼" mark; backstitch. Stitch in the direction of the arrow all the way to the outer edge.

2. Sew a second diamond to the triangle, starting at the ¼" mark on the inner point; backstitch. Stitch in the direction of the arrow to the outer edge.

3. Match the points of the diamonds and sew them together, starting at the inner ¼" mark. Press this seam to one side and press the seams on the triangle toward the diamonds.

4. Sew a square to a diamond unit. Begin stitching at the ¼" mark; backstitch. Stitch in the direction of the arrow all the way to the outer edge.

5. Sew a second diamond unit to the square. Begin stitching at the ¼" mark; backstitch. Stitch in the direction of the arrow all the way to the outer edge.

6. Match the point of the diamonds and sew them together, starting at the inner ¼" mark. Press this seam to one side and press the seams on the square toward the diamonds.

7. Sew the sides of the large diamond units to adjacent sides of 1 square. Begin stitching at the ¼" mark; backstitch. Stitch in the direction of the arrow all the way to the outer edge. Repeat with the remaining square.

8. Match the center points and pin. Stitch from mark to mark. Press the center seam to one side and press the seams of the squares toward the diamonds.

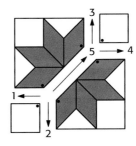

Liberty Star

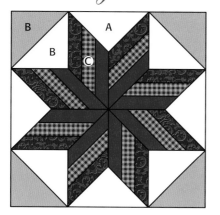

Cutting

Fabric	Piece	Cut
1	C	1 strip, 1⅜" x 42"
3	B	2 squares, 4⅜" x 4⅜"; cut once diagonally to yield 4 half-square triangles
4	C	1 strip, 1⅜" x 42"
6	C	1 strip, 1⅜" x 42"
8	A	1 square, 6¼" x 6¼"; cut twice diagonally to yield 4 quarter-square triangles
8	B	2 squares, 4⅜" x 4⅜"; cut once diagonally to yield 4 half-square triangles

Block Assembly

1. Sew the 1⅜"-wide C strips together, staggering the seams about 1". Align the 45° line on the ruler with a horizontal seam and cut one end at a 45° angle.

2. Cut 8 segments, 3" wide, from the strip unit, making each cut parallel to the first cut.

Diamond Unit
Cut 8.

3. Sew a background triangle (B) and a Fabric #3 triangle (B) together to make the corner units.

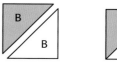

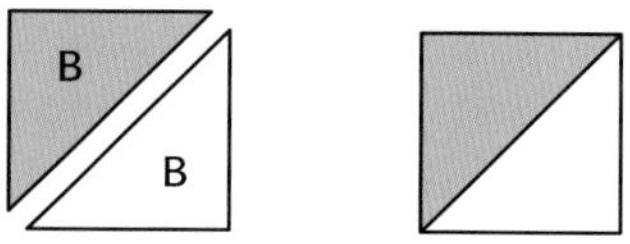

Corner Unit
Make 4.

4. Arrange the diamond units, triangles (A), and corner units (B/B). Sew the units together, following the directions on page 89 for constructing an eight-pointed star.

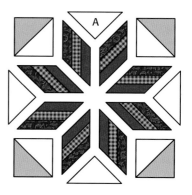

Castle Keep

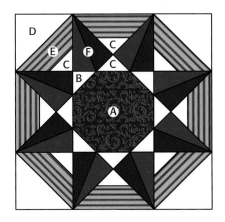

Cutting

Fabric	Piece	Cut
1	A	1 square, 5½" x 5½"
2	F	1 strip, 2" x 42"
4	F	1 strip, 2" x 42"
7	E	2 squares, 6¼" x 6¼"; cut twice diagonally to yield 8 quarter-square triangles
8	B	4 squares, 2" x 2"
8	C	6 squares, 2⅜" x 2⅜"; cut once diagonally to yield 12 half-square triangles
8	D	2 squares, 4⅜" x 4⅜"; cut once diagonally to yield 4 half-square triangles

Block Assembly

1. Mark a diagonal line on the wrong side of each small background square (B). Place a marked square on a corner of the large Fabric #1 square (A). Stitch on the diagonal line and trim the seam allowance to ¼". Press the triangle toward the corner. Repeat with the remaining marked squares on the other 3 corners of the large square.

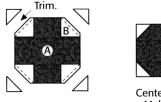

Center Unit
Make 1.

2. To make a trapezoid (E), place the ruler's 2" mark on the long edge of a Fabric #7 quarter-square triangle. Use a rotary cutter to trim the corner.

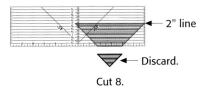

2" line

Discard.

Cut 8.

3. Sew a small background triangle (C) to the short side of a Fabric #7 trapezoid (E). To each of 4 E/C units, sew a large background triangle (D) to make a corner unit. Press the seams toward the trapezoid. Use the remaining 4 (E/C) units for the side triangles.

Side Triangle
Make 8.

Corner Unit
Make 4.

4. With right sides together, sew the Fabric #2 and Fabric #4 F strips together on both long edges, using a ¼"-wide seam allowance.

5. Make a paper template of the Castle Keep cutting guide on page 95; mark the grain line and seam lines. Place the corner of the template on the underside corner of a ruler; tape in place.

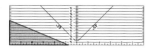

6. With the wrong side of the Fabric #4 strip face up, place the edge of the template on one edge of the strip unit. Cut along both edges of the ruler. To cut the next segment, rotate the ruler so the edge of the template is on the opposite long edge of the strip unit; trim. Continue rotating the ruler from one long edge to the other to cut 6 more segments.

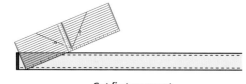

Cut first segment.

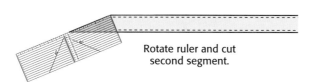

Rotate ruler and cut second segment.

7. Carefully undo the stitching at the point of each segment. Press the seam open and trim away any tips extending beyond the edge.

Undo stitching.

Piece F
Make 8.

8. Sew a side triangle (C/E unit) to the Fabric #2 side of piece F.

Make 4.

9. Sew the short side of a background triangle (C) to the Fabric #4 short edge of piece F.

Make 4.

10. Join the units made in steps 8 and 9 together to complete the side units.

Side Unit
Make 4.

11. Arrange the center unit, side units, and corner units. Sew the units together in horizontal rows. Join the rows to complete the block.

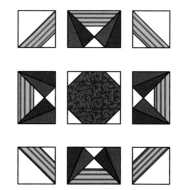

Twinkling Star

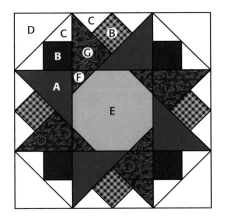

Cutting

Fabric	Piece	Cut
1	F	4 squares, 2" x 2"
1	G	2 squares, 4⅜" x 4⅜"; cut once diagonally to yield 4 half-square triangles
2	B	4 squares, 2¼" x 2¼"
3	E	1 square, 5½" x 5½"
4	A	2 squares, 4⅜" x 4⅜"; cut once diagonally to yield 4 half-square triangles
6	B	4 squares, 2¼" x 2¼"
8	C	4 squares, 3¾" x 3¾"; cut twice diagonally to yield 16 quarter-square triangles
8	D	2 squares, 4⅜" x 4⅜"; cut once diagonally to yield 4 half-square triangles

Block Assembly

1. Sew the short side of 2 background triangles (C) to a Fabric #6 square (B).

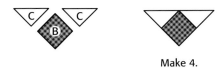

Make 4.

2. To cut piece G, place the corner of a ruler on a Fabric #1 triangle so that the ruler's 4⅜" mark is on the left-hand point of the triangle and the top edge of the ruler is even with the top of the triangle. Cut along the edge of the ruler to trim the corner of the triangle.

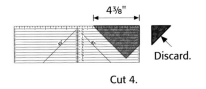

Discard.

Cut 4.

3. Sew piece G to the left side of a unit made in step 1. Sew this unit to a large Fabric #4 triangle (A).

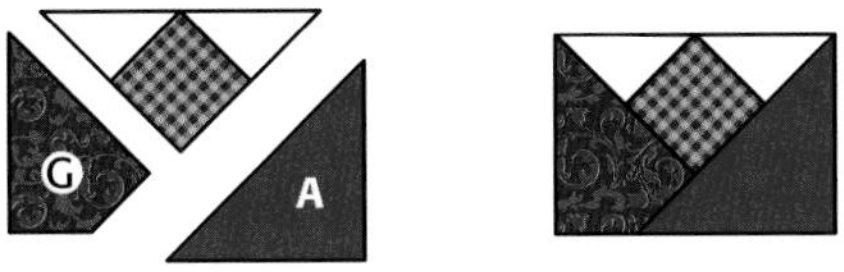

Side Unit
Make 4.

4. Sew the short side of 2 background triangles (C) to a Fabric #2 square (B). Sew this unit to a large background triangle (D) to make a corner unit.

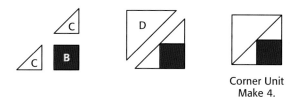

Corner Unit
Make 4.

5. Mark a diagonal line on the wrong side of each small Fabric #1 square (F). Place a marked square on a corner of the large Fabric #3 square (E). Stitch on the diagonal line and trim the seam allowance to ¼". Press the triangle toward the corner. Repeat with the remaining marked squares on the other 3 corners.

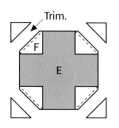

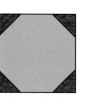

Center Unit
Make 1.

6. Arrange the center unit, side units, and corner units. Sew the units together into horizontal rows. Join the rows to complete the block.

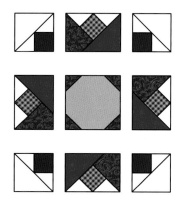

Quilt Assembly and Finishing

1. Arrange the blocks on-point. Position the sashing strips and cornerstones around the blocks. Sew the sashing strips between the blocks and at the end of each row. Sew the sashing strips and cornerstones together to make sashing rows.

2. Sew the sashing rows and rows of blocks together. Add the side triangles to the ends of the rows.

3. Join the rows, adding the corner triangles last.

4. Referring to "Straight-Cut Borders" on pages 11–12, measure, trim, and sew the inner border strips to the side edges of the quilt top first, then to the top and bottom edges. Repeat for the outer border strips.
5. Layer the quilt top with batting and backing; baste. Quilt as desired.
6. Bind the edges and add a label.

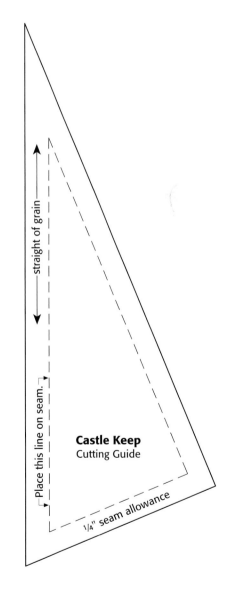

straight of grain

Place this line on seam.

Castle Keep
Cutting Guide

¼" seam allowance

Books from Martingale & Company

Appliqué
Appliqué in Bloom
Baltimore Bouquets
Basic Quiltmaking Techniques for Hand Appliqué
Basic Quiltmaking Techniques for Machine Appliqué
Coxcomb Quilt
The Easy Art of Appliqué
Folk Art Animals
From a Quilter's Garden
Fun with Sunbonnet Sue
Garden Appliqué
Interlacing Borders
Once Upon a Quilt
Stars in the Garden
Sunbonnet Sue All Through the Year
Welcome to the North Pole

Basic Quiltmaking Techniques
Basic Quiltmaking Techniques for Borders & Bindings
Basic Quiltmaking Techniques for Curved Piecing
Basic Quiltmaking Techniques for Divided Circles
Basic Quiltmaking Techniques for Eight-Pointed Stars
Basic Quiltmaking Techniques for Hand Appliqué
Basic Quiltmaking Techniques for Machine Appliqué
Basic Quiltmaking Techniques for Strip Piecing
Your First Quilt Book (or it should be!)

Crafts
15 Beads
The Art of Handmade Paper and Collage
Christmas Ribbonry
Fabric Mosaics
Folded Fabric Fun
Hand-Stitched Samplers from I Done My Best
The Home Decorator's Stamping Book
Making Memories
A Passion for Ribbonry
Stamp with Style

Design Reference
Color: The Quilter's Guide
Design Essentials: The Quilter's Guide
Design Your Own Quilts
The Nature of Design
QuiltSkills
Surprising Designs from Traditional Quilt Blocks

Foundation/Paper Piecing
Classic Quilts with Precise Foundation Piecing
Crazy but Pieceable
Easy Machine Paper Piecing
Easy Mix & Match Machine Paper Piecing
Easy Paper-Pieced Keepsake Quilts
Easy Paper-Pieced Miniatures
Easy Reversible Vests
Go Wild with Quilts
Go Wild with Quilts—Again!
It's Raining Cats & Dogs
Mariner's Medallion
Paper Piecing the Seasons
A Quilter's Ark
Sewing on the Line
Show Me How to Paper Piece

Home Decorating
Decorate with Quilts & Collections
The Home Decorator's Stamping Book
Living with Little Quilts
Make Room for Quilts
Special-Occasion Table Runners
Stitch & Stencil
Welcome Home: Debbie Mumm
Welcome Home: Kaffe Fassett

Joy of Quilting Series
Borders by Design
The Easy Art of Appliqué
A Fine Finish

Hand-Dyed Fabric Made Easy
Happy Endings
Loving Stitches
Machine Quilting Made Easy
A Perfect Match
Press for Success
Sensational Settings
Shortcuts
The Ultimate Book of Quilt Labels

Knitting
Simply Beautiful Sweaters
Two Sticks and a String
Welcome Home: Kaffe Fassett

Machine Quilting/Sewing
Machine Needlelace
Machine Quilting Made Easy
Machine Quilting with Decorative Threads
Quilting Makes the Quilt
Thread Magic
Threadplay

Miniature/Small Quilts
Celebrate! with Little Quilts
Crazy but Pieceable
Easy Paper-Pieced Miniatures
Fun with Miniature Log Cabin Blocks
Little Quilts All Through the House
Living with Little Quilts
Miniature Baltimore Album Quilts
Small Quilts Made Easy
Small Wonders

Quilting/Finishing Techniques
Borders by Design
The Border Workbook
A Fine Finish
Happy Endings
Interlacing Borders
Loving Stitches
Quilt It!
Quilting Design Sourcebook
Quilting Makes the Quilt
Traditional Quilts with Painless Borders
The Ultimate Book of Quilt Labels

Rotary Cutting/Speed Piecing
101 Fabulous Rotary-Cut Quilts
All-Star Sampler
Around the Block with Judy Hopkins
Bargello Quilts
Basic Quiltmaking Techniques for Strip Piecing
Block by Block
Easy Seasonal Wall Quilts
Easy Star Sampler
Fat Quarter Quilts
The Heirloom Quilt
The Joy of Quilting
More Quilts for Baby
More Strip-Pieced Watercolor Magic
A New Slant on Bargello Quilts
A New Twist on Triangles
Patchwork Pantry
Quilters on the Go
Quilting Up a Storm
Quilts for Baby
Quilts from Aunt Amy
ScrapMania
Simply Scrappy Quilts
Square Dance
Strip-Pieced Watercolor Magic
Stripples Strikes Again!
Strips That Sizzle
Two-Color Quilts

Seasonal Projects
Christmas Ribbonry
Easy Seasonal Wall Quilts

Folded Fabric Fun
Holiday Happenings
Quilted for Christmas
Quilted for Christmas, Book III
Quilted for Christmas, Book IV
A Silk-Ribbon Album
Welcome to the North Pole

Stitchery/Needle Arts
Christmas Ribbonry
Crazy Rags
Hand-Stitched Samplers from I Done My Best
Machine Needlelace
Miniature Baltimore Album Quilts
A Passion for Ribbonry
A Silk-Ribbon Album
Victorian Elegance

Surface Design/Fabric Manipulation
15 Beads
The Art of Handmade Paper and Collage
Complex Cloth
Creative Marbling on Fabric
Dyes & Paints
Hand-Dyed Fabric Made Easy
Jazz It Up

Theme Quilts
The Cat's Meow
Everyday Angels in Extraordinary Quilts
Fabric Collage Quilts
Fabric Mosaics
Folded Fabric Fun
Folk Art Quilts
Honoring the Seasons
It's Raining Cats & Dogs
Life in the Country with Country Threads
Making Memories
More Quilts for Baby
The Nursery Rhyme Quilt
Once Upon a Quilt
Patchwork Pantry
Quilted Landscapes
Quilting Your Memories
Quilts for Baby
Quilts from Nature
Through the Window and Beyond
Two-Color Quilts

Watercolor Quilts
More Strip-Pieced Watercolor Magic
Strip-Pieced Watercolor Magic
Watercolor Impressions
Watercolor Quilts

Wearables
Crazy Rags
Dress Daze
Easy Reversible Vests
Jacket Jazz Encore
Just Like Mommy
Variations in Chenille

Many of these books are available through your local quilt, fabric, craft-supply, or art-supply store. For more information, call, write, fax, or e-mail for our free full-color catalog.

Martingale & Company
PO Box 118
Bothell, WA 98041-0118 USA
1-800-426-3126
International: 1-425-483-3313
24-Hour Fax: 1-425-486-7596
Web site: www.patchwork.com
E-mail: info@martingale-pub.com

3/99